CONFERDERATE POETS
Volume I

Portraits:

Top Left: Margaret Junkin Preston

Top Right: Columbus Drew

Center: Francis Orray Ticknor

Bottom Left: John Reuben Thompson

Bottom Right: Mary Bayard Devereux Clarke

The Land They Loved:
Volume II

CONFEDERATE
Poets & Poems
Volume 1

Edited by
Clyde N. Wilson

Produced in the Republic of South Carolina by

SHOTWELL PUBLISHING LLC

Post Office Box 2592

Columbia, So. Carolina 29202

www.ShotwellPublishing.com

Cover design: Boo Jackson. Portraits are public domain.

ISBN: 978-1-963506-18-1

FIRST EDITION

10 9 8 7 6 5 4 3 2

CONTENTS

FOREWORD, ix

I. WELCOMING INDEPENDENCE

DIXIE, 3

THE BONNIE BLUE FLAG, 6

SAMUEL HENRY DICKSON

South Carolina, 10

"ST. GEORGE TUCKER, OF VIRGINIA"

The Southern Cross, 12

BREWTON MARTIN ANDERSON

The New Star, 14

THE FIRE OF FREEDOM, 16

AUGUSTUS JULIAN REQUIER

Our Faith in '61, 18

JOHN WILFORD OVERALL

Seventy-Six And Sixty-One, 21

"CAROLINE"

Farewell to Brother Jonathan, 23

JAMES BARRON HOPE

The Oath of Freedom, 26

THE BLESSED UNION, 30

JOHN KILLUM

Old Betsy, 31

A PRAYER FOR OUR ENEMIES, 32

II. POETS FOR THE DURATION

MARY BAYARD DEVEREUX CLARKE

The Rebel Sock, 35

His Last Word, 39

General Lee at The Battle of The Wilderness, 40

JANE TANDY CROSS

Over the River, 42

The Confederacy, 44

President Davis, 46

COLUMBUS DREW

Uncle Sam, 48

The Grey-Clad Partisan, 51

Camp Song of the St. Augustine Confederate, 52

The Last Look of the Dying Soldier, 56

All Quiet Upon The Olustee To-Night, 58

Only A Tramp, 61

Song of The Spinning Wheel, 63

PAUL HAMILTON HAYNE

Charleston, 64

Vicksburg — A Ballad, 67

Sonnet, 69

Addressed to Henry Timrod, Esq., 70

EMILY J. MOORE

The Salkehatchie, 71

Tell The Boys The War Is Ended, 73

ALBERT PIKE

Dixie to Arms!, 75

The Magnolia, 78

MARGARET JUNKIN PRESTON

Hymn to The National Flag, 80

The Shade of The Trees, 82

Only A Private, 84

JAMES RYDER RANDALL

Maryland, My Maryland, 86

John Pelham, 90

At Fort Pillow, 92

WILLIAM GILMORE SIMMS

The Irrepressible Conflict, 96

Sonnet, 97

Sonnet—The Ship of State, 98

The Avatar of Hell, 99

Battle Hymn, 100

The Mountain Partisan, 101

Ode—Our City By The Sea, 103

Fort Wagner, 105

Not Doubtful of Your Fatherland, 107

Sacrifice, 109

South Carolina, 110

CARRIE BELLE SINCLAIR

The Homespun Dress, 112

Georgia, My Georgia!, 116

HENRY THROOP STANTON

The Bivouac, 118

The Little Boy Guiding the Plow, 121

OLIVIA TULLY THOMAS

The Southern Republic, 124

When Peace Returns, 127

JOHN REUBEN THOMPSON

The Burial of Latane', 129

Coercion: A Poem for Then and Now, 132

On to Richmond, 135

A Farewell to Pope, 141

MERIWETHER "JEFF" THOMPSON

Missouri, Missouri, Awake from Thy Slumber, 143

A Rebel, 144

Damn It, Let It Rip, 145

FRANCIS ORRAY TICKNOR

Home, Sweet Home, 146

The Old Rifleman, 147

Little Giffen, 149

Our Left, 151

Loyal, 153

The Virginians of The Valley, 155

HENRY TIMROD

Ora Pace, 156

Ethnogenesis, 157

A Cry to Arm, 164

Carolina, 166

The Two Armies, 170

Christmas, 172

Charleston, 176

Address Delivered at the Opening of the New Theatre at Richmond, 178

Hymn, 183

Carmen Triumphale, 184

III. ENGLISH FRIENDS

WILLIAM ERNEST HENLEY

Romance, 189

PHILIP STANHOPE WORSLEY

Thy Troy Has Fallen, 191

SIR HENRY HOUGHTON

A Reply to "The Conquered Banner", 193

ABOUT THE EDITOR, 195

Foreword

THIS COLLECTION OF VERSE is made, not from the viewpoint of a literary critic, but that of a student of history interested in how the experiences of the Southern people have been reflected in verse. Poetry conveys a kind of truth not found in other forms of human discourse. The father of Southern literature, William Gilmore Simms, made the relevant point in the preface to his *War Poetry of the South*:

> The emotional literature of a people is as necessary to the philosophical historian as the mere details of events in the progress of a nation. This is essential to the reputation of the Southern people, as illustrating their feelings, sentiments, ideas and opinions—the motives which influenced their actions, and the objects which they had in contemplation, and which seemed to them to justify the struggle in which they were engaged.

And what a struggle. The fashionable historians have satisfied themselves that anything that is said in defense of the Southern people in their great trial by fire is merely a "Lost Cause Mythology" made up after the fact to justify Southerners' evil and failed rebellion. The same historians are now smirkingly busy making a phony case that the South did not really suffer all that much under the benevolent Northern invasion and subsequent Reconstruction, that Southern claims of harm are exaggerated.

It is plain fact that no large group of Americans has fought so bravely and skillfully, with such dedication, sacrifice, and suffering as did the Confederate people. That should be kept in mind while reading this volume presenting the "feelings, sentiments, ideas, and opinions" of those who expressed themselves in verse under the highest hopes, severest trials, and deepest loss.

The Confederacy was fighting an invading power of four times its size with access to all the resources of the world. Southern men were mobilised to an extent never matched in American history, and in the end nearly a quarter perished. In 1864 Tennessee and Kentucky were occupied and the Mississippi blocked. New Orleans was gone and Richmond and Charleston were under heavy siege. A considerable part of the civil population, including black people, had seen their shelter, food, and livings deliberately destroyed. Yet the people, including the women, remained game and continued to defeat larger forces.

Foreign visitors remarked that in Northern cities they saw no signs of war except for busy contractors. Could the North have kept up a war if, instead of a prosperous home front and vast sums spent on enlistment bounties, Chicago and Philadelphia were occupied and Boston under siege? With large parts of Pennsylvania and Ohio overrun and devastated?

Confederate verse that has been gathered by collectors would fill several large volumes. Who knows how much perished in the newspapers of the time, which was the main outlet for verse? Much of it, like that of the North, is too sentimental for us, but not all. Some represents the serious thought and art of an incubating civilisation aborted. We have looked for the best works of the best poets, and for indications of the Southern people's experience as described by Simms.

In reading Confederate verse it might be useful to recall now and then the opposition's ideas and sentiments as exhibited in "The Battle Hymn of the Republic," "We are Coming, Father Abraham," or the childish jingles of Walt Whitman. Of course, formal verse does not have the power of music to create emotion and memory. One cannot ignore the large treasury of Confederate music. In this and the next volume we have included a selection of song lyrics. Indeed, poems were sometimes set to music for songs that became popular, some of them beloved even by the other side. To immerse yourself in Confederate music you can do no better than listen to the six discs of Bobby Horton's "Homespun Songs of the C.S.A."

There are many good renditions by other groups, notably the 2nd South Carolina String Band.

Henry Timrod in an essay on Southern literature pointed out that Southern writing in his time had not quite reached universal and timeless status. Certainly Poe, Simms, and Timrod himself as well as certain prose writers show evidence of a maturing Southern culture that would achieve undoubted universal status in the 20th century. The old canard about the supposed intellectual inferiority of the antebellum South has been fully refuted by historians. Like Ireland, the soul of the South survived brutal suppression in its youth.

Volume 2 of *Confederate Poets and Poems* (Vol. 3 of *The Land They Loved*) will include many more war poems, spirited or sad, by many other Southern writers. Also, poets who dealt with defeat and loss.

Studying these verses will establish beyond a doubt that Confederates were learned and thoughtful people and that the Lost Cause was a great deal more than a Myth.

What shall we say who have knowledge carried to
the heart?

—Allen Tate, "Ode to the Confederate Dead"

I. Welcoming Independence

"DIXIE" was composed shortly before The War by the Yankee Daniel Emmett for his black-face minstrel show. Such shows were written, produced and acted by Northerners for Northern audiences. In high spirits the South captured the tune and made it the most rousing national anthem of any people. The French and the Welsh have pretty good ones, but ours is the best and expresses our love of homeland perfectly.

Dixie

I wish I was in de land ob cotton,

Old times dar am not forgotten,

Look away, look away, look away, Dixie land,

In Dixie land, whar I was born in,

Early on one frosty mornin',

Look away, look away, look away, Dixie land,

Den I wish I was in Dixie,

Hooray, hooray,

In Dixie land I'll take my stand

To lib an' die in Dixie,

Away, away, away down South in Dixie.

Away, away, away down South in Dixie.

Ole Missus marry Will-de-weaber,

William was a gay deceaber,

Look away, look away, look away, Dixie land.

But when he put his arm around 'er,

He smiled as fierce as a forty-pounder,

Look away, look away, look away, Dixie land.

Den I wish I was in Dixie,
Hooray, hooray,
In Dixie land I'll take my stand
To lib an' die in Dixie,
Away, away, away down South in Dixie.
Away, away, away down South in Dixie.

His face was sharp as a butcher's cleaber,
But dat it did not seem to greab 'er,
Look away, look away, look away, Dixie land.

Den I wish I was in Dixie,
Hooray, hooray,
In Dixie land I'll take my stand
To lib an' die in Dixie,
Away, away, away down South in Dixie.
Away, away, away down South in Dixie.

Dere's buckwheat cakes and Injun batter,
Makes you fat or a little fatter,
Look away, look away, look away, Dixie land.
Den hoe it down an' scratch your grabbel,
To Dixie land I'm bound to trabble,
Look away, look away, look away, Dixie land.

Den I wish I was in Dixie,

Hooray, hooray,

In Dixie land I'll take my stand

To lib an' die in Dixie,

Away, away, away down South in Dixie.

Away, away, away down South in Dixie.

♦ ♦ ♦

"THE BONNIE BLUE FLAG!" The flag of the song was a blue one with a white, or sometimes gold, star in the center. It was used by Americans in the Spanish colony of West Florida (the coast areas of Alabama and Mississippi) in declaring independence in 1810. It was a popular symbol of secession and flew over the Mississippi capitol. The rousing song remained popular even when the flag became less prominent. The author was Irish-born Harry McCarthy (d. 1874). His troupe travelled over the South with his sister or wife singing to large crowds. During his occupation of New Orleans, the Yankee General Beast Butler seized the plates from the publisher and threatened to punish anyone whistling the song.

The Bonnie Blue Flag

We are a band of brothers,

And native to the soil,

Fighting for the property

We gained by honest toil;

And when our rights were threatened,

The cry rose near and far—

"Hurrah for the Bonnie Blue Flag

That bears the single star!"

Hurrah, hurrah!

For Southern Rights, hurrah!

Hurrah for the Bonnie Blue Flag

That bears a single star.

As long as the Union

Was faithful to her trust,

Like friends and like brothers

Both kind were we and just;
But now, when Northern treachery
Attempts our rights to mar,
We hoist the Bonnie Blue Flag
That bears a single star.

    Hurrah, hurrah!
    For Southern Rights, hurrah!
    Hurrah for the Bonnie Blue Flag
    That bears a single star.

First gallant South Carolina
Nobly made the stand,
Then came Alabama,
Who took her by the hand;
Next quickly Mississippi,
Georgia and Florida,
All raised on high the Bonnie Blue Flag,
That bears a single Star.

    Hurrah, hurrah!
    For Southern Rights, hurrah!
    Hurrah for the Bonnie Blue Flag
    That bears a single star.

Ye men of valour gather round the banner of right.
Texas and fair Louisiana join us in the fight,

Davis our loved President, and Stephens statesman rare,
Now rally round the Bonnie Blue Flag
    that bears a single star.

    Hurrah, hurrah!
    For Southern Rights, hurrah!
    Hurrah for the Bonnie Blue Flag
    That bears a single star.

And here's to old Virginia—
The Old Dominion State—
With the Young Confed' racy
At length has linked her fate,
Impelled by her example,
Now other states prepare
To hoist on high the Bonnie Blue Flag
that bears a single Star.

    Hurrah, hurrah!
    For Southern Rights, hurrah!
    Hurrah for the Bonnie Blue Flag
    That bears a single star.

Then cheer, boys, cheer;
Raise the joyous shout,
For Arkansas and North Carolina

Now have both gone out;
And let another rousing cheer
For Tennessee be given,
The single star of the Bonnie Blue Flag
Has grown to be eleven.

Hurrah, hurrah!
For Southern Rights, hurrah!
Hurrah for the Bonnie Blue Flag
That bears a single star.

Then here's to our Confed'racy,
Strong are we and brave,
Like patriots of old we'll fight
Our heritage to save.
And rather than submit to shame,
To die we would prefer;
So cheer for the Bonnie Blue Flag
That bears the single star.

Hurrah, hurrah!
For Southern Rights, hurrah!
Hurrah for the Bonnie Blue Flag
That bears a single star.

♦ ♦ ♦

SAMUEL HENRY DICKSON (1798—1872), of South Carolina was a physician noted for his advanced scientific knowledge as a writer and lecturer. When he wrote, or shortly before, he was serving as a professor at America's foremost medical school in Philadelphia.

South Carolina, December 20, 1860

The deed is done! the die is cast;
The glorious Rubicon is passed:
Hail, Carolina! free at last!

Strong in the right, I see her stand
Where ocean laves the shelving sand;
Her own Palmetto decks the strand.

She turns aloft her flashing eye;
Radiant, her lonely star on high
Shines clear amidst the darkening sky.

Silent, along those azure deeps
Its course her silver crescent keeps,
And in soft light the landscape steeps.

Fling forth her banner to the gale!
Let all the hosts of earth assail,—
Their fury and their force shall fail.

Echoes the wide resounding shore,
With voice above th' Atlantic roar,
Her sons proclaim her free once more!

Oh, land of heroes! Spartan State!
In numbers few, in daring great,
Thus to affront the frowns of fate!

And while mad triumph rules the hour,
And thickening clouds of menace lower,
Bear back the tide of tyrant power.

With steadfast courage, faltering never,
Sternly resolved, her bonds we sever:
Hail, Carolina! Free forever!

♦ ♦ ♦

"ST. GEORGE TUCKER, OF VIRGINIA." The unknown writer of this verse apparently used as pseudonym the name of the Revolutionary hero and constitutional authority St. George Tucker, who died in 1827.

The Southern Cross

OH! say can you see, through the gloom and the storm,

More bright for the darkness, that pure constellation!

Like the symbol of love and redemption its form,

As it points to the haven of hope for the nation.

Now radiant each star, as the beacon afar,

Giving promise of peace, or assurance in war,

'Tis the Cross of the South, which shall ever remain

To light us to freedom and glory again!

How peaceful and blest was America's soil.

'Till betrayed by the guile of the Puritan demon,

Which lurks under virtue, and springs from its coil

To fasten its fangs in the life-blood, of freemen.

Then boldly appeal to each heart that can feel,

And crush the foul viper 'neath Liberty's heel!

And the Cross of the South shall in triumph remain,

To light us to freedom and glory again!

'Tis the emblem of peace, 'tis the day—star of hope,

Like the sacred Labarum that guided the Roman;

From the shores of the Gulf to the Delaware's slope,

'Tis the trust of the free, and the terror of foemen.

Fling its folds to the air, while we boldly declare

The rights we demand or the deeds that we dare!

While the Cross of the South shall in triumph remain,

To light us to freedom and glory again!

And if peace should be hopeless and justice denied,

And war's bloody vulture should flap its black pinions,

Then gladly "to arms," while we hurl, in our pride,

Defiance to tyrants and death to their minions!

With our front in the field, swearing never to yield,

Or return, like the Spartan, in death on our shield!

And the Cross of the South shall triumphantly wave,

As the flag of the free, or the pall of the brave!

♦ ♦ ♦

BREWTON MARTIN ANDERSON

The New Star

Another star arisen; another flag unfurled;
Another name inscribed among the nations of the world;
Another mighty struggle 'gainst a tyrant's fell decree,
And again a burdened people have uprisen, and are free.

The spirit of the fathers in the children liveth yet;
Liveth still the olden blood which dimmed the foreign bayonet;
And the fathers fought for freedom, and the sons for freedom fight;
Their God was with the fathers—and is still the God of right!

Behold! the skies are darkened! A gloomy cloud hath lowered!
Shall it break before the sun of peace, or spread in rage impowered?
Shall we have the smile of friendship, or shall it be the blow?
Shall it be the right hand to the friend, or the red hand to the foe?

In peacefulness we wish to live, but not in slavish fear;
In peacefulness we dare not die, dishonoured on our bier.
To our allies of the Northern land we offer heart and hand,
But if they scorn our friendship—then the banner and the brand!

Honour to the new-born nation! and honour to the brave!

A country freed from thralldom, or a soldier's honoured grave.

Every step shall be contested; every rivulet run red,

And the invader, should he conquer, find the conquered in the dead.

But victory shall follow where the sons of freedom go,

And the signal for the onset be the death—knell of the foe;

And hallowed shall the spot be where he was so bravely met,

And the star which yonder rises, rises never more to set.

♦ ♦ ♦

"THE FIRE OF FREEDOM." An unknown writer in the Charleston *Mercury*.

The Fire of Freedom

The holy fire that nerved the Greek
To make his stand at Marathon,
Until the last red foeman's shriek
Proclaimed that freedom's fight was won,
Still lives unquenched—unquenchable:
Through every age its fires will burn—
Lives in the hermit's lonely cell,
And springs from every storied urn.

The hearthstone embers hold the spark
Where fell oppression's foot hath trod;
Through superstition's shadow dark
It flashes to the living God!
From Moscow's ashes springs the Russ;
In Warsaw, Poland lives again:
Schamyl, on frosty Caucasus,
Strikes liberty's electric chain!

Tell's freedom-beacon lights the Swiss;
Vainly the invader ever strives;
He finds *Sic Semper Tyranis*
In San Jacinto's bowie-knives!

Than these—than all—a holier fire
Now burns thy soul, Virginia's son!
Strike then for wife, babe, gray-haired sire,
Strike for the grave of Washington!

The Northern rabble arms for greed;
The hireling parson goads the train—
In that foul crop from bigot seed,
Old "Praise God Barebones" howls again!
We welcome them to "Southern lands,"
We welcome them to "Southern slaves,"
We welcome them "with bloody hands
To hospitable Southern graves!"

♦ ♦ ♦

AUGUSTUS JULIAN REOUIER (1825—1887) of Alabama was a Mobile attorney.

Our Faith in '61

"That governments are instituted among men, deriving their just powers from the consent of the governed: that whenever any form of government becomes destructive of these ends, it is the right of the people to alter or abolish it, and to institute a new government, laying its foundation on such principles, and organizing its powers in such form, as TO THEM SHALL SEEM most likely to effect their safety and happiness." –Declaration of Independence, July 4, '76

Not yet one hundred years have flown
Since on this very spot,
The subjects of a sovereign throne—
Liege-master of their lot—
This high degree sped o'er the sea,
From council-board and tent,
"No earthly power can rule the free
But by their own consent!"

For this, they fought as Saxons fight,
On bloody fields and long—
Themselves the champions of the right,
And judges of the wrong;
For this their stainless knighthood wore
The branded rebel's name,
Until the starry cross they bore
Set all the skies aflame!

And States co-equal and distinct
Outshone the western sun,
By one great charter interlinked—
Not blended into one;
Whose graven key that high decree
The grand inscription lent,
"No earthly power can rule the free
But by their own consent!"

Oh! sordid age! Oh! ruthless rage!
Oh! sacrilegious wrong!
A deed to blast the record page,
And snap the strings of song;
In that great charter's name, a band
By groveling greed enticed,
Whose warrant is the grasping hand
Of creeds without a Christ—

States that have trampled every pledge
Its crystal code contains,
Now give their swords a keener edge
To harness it with chains—
To make a bond of brotherhood
The sanction and the seal,
By which to arm a rabble brood
With fratricidal steel.

Who, conscious that their cause is black,
In puling prose and rhyme,
Talk hatefully of love, and tack
Hypocrisy to crime;
Who smile and smite, engross the gorge
Or impotently frown;
And call us "rebels" with King George,
As if they wore his crown!

Most venal of a venal race,
Who think you cheat the sky
With every pharisaic face
And simulated lie;
Round Freedom's lair, with weapons bare,
We greet the light divine
Of those who throned the goddess there,
And yet inspire the shrine!

Our loved ones' graves are at our feet,
Their homesteads at our back—
No belted Southron can retreat
With women on his track;
Peal, bannered host, the proud decree
Which from your fathers went,
"No earthly power can rule the free
But by their own consent!"

♦ ♦ ♦

JOHN WILFORD OVERALL (1822—1899) of Louisiana was a lawyer and journalist in New Orleans and other Southern cities, and from 1876 in New York.

Seventy-Six And Sixty-One

Ye spirits of the glorious dead!

Ye watchers in the sky!

Who sought the patriot's crimson bed,

With holy trust and high—

Come, lend your inspiration now,

Come, fire each Southern son,

Who nobly fights for freemen's rights,

And shouts for sixty-one.

Come, teach them how, on hill or glade,

Quick leaping from your side,

The lightning flash of sabres made

A red and flowing tide—

How well ye fought, how bravely fell,

Beneath our burning sun;

And let the lyre, in strains of fire,

So speak of sixty-one.

There's many a grave in all the land,

And many a crucifix,

Which tells how that heroic band

Stood firm in seventy-six—

Ye heroes of the deathless past,

Your glorious race is run,
But from your dust springs freemen's trust.
And blows for sixty-one.

We build our altars where you lie,
On many a verdant sod,
With sabres pointing to the sky,
And sanctified of God;
The smoke shall rise from every pile,
Till freedom's cause is won,
And every mouth throughout the South,
Shall shout for sixty-one!

♦ ♦ ♦

"CAROLINE." Brother Jonathan was a nickname for New Englanders. The cold refusal is a reference to New England's lack of patriotism in the War of 1812.

Farewell to Brother Jonathan

Farewell! we must part; we have turned from the land

Of our cold-hearted brother, with tyrannous hand,

Who assumed all our rights as a favor to grant,

And whose smile ever covered the sting of a taunt;

Who breathed on the fame he was bound to defend,—

Still the craftiest foe, 'neath the guise of a friend;

Who believed that our bosoms would bleed at a touch,

Yet could never believe he could goad them too much;

Whose conscience affects to be seared with our sin,

Yet is plastic to take all its benefits in;

The mote in our eye so enormous has grown,

That he never perceives there's a beam in his own.

O, Jonathan, Jonathan! vassal of pelf,

Self-righteous, self-glorious, yes, every inch self,

Your loyalty now is all bluster and boast,

But was dumb when the foemen invaded our coast.

In vain did your country appeal to you then,
You coldly refused her your money and men;
Your trade interrupted, you slunk from her wars,
And preferred British gold to the Stripes and the Stars!

Then our generous blood was as water poured forth,
And the sons of the South were the shields of the North;
Nor our patriot ardor one moment gave o'er,
Till the foe you had fed we had driven from the shore!

Long years we have suffered opprobrium and wrong,
But we clung to your side with affection so strong,
That at last, in mere wanton aggression, you broke
All the ties of our hearts with one murderous stroke.

We are tired of contest for what is our own,
We are sick of a strife that could never be done;
Thus our love has died out, and its altars are dark,
Not Prometheus's self could rekindle the spark.

O Jonathan, Jonathan! deadly the sin
Of your tigerish thirst for the blood of your kin;
And shameful the spirit that gloats over wives
And maidens despoiled of their honour and lives!

Your palaces rise from the fruits of our toil.

Your millions are fed from the wealth of our soil;

The balm of our air brings the health to your cheek,

And our hearts are aglow with the welcome we speak.

O brother! beware how you seek us again,

Lest you brand on your forehead the signet of Cain;

That blood and that crime on your conscience must sit;

We may fall—we may perish—but never submit!

The pathway that leads to the Pharisee's door

We remember, indeed, but we tread it no more;

Preferring to turn, with the Publican's faith,

To the path through the valley and shadow of death!

♦ ♦ ♦

JAMES BARRON HOPE (1827—1887) of Virginia was a member of a prominent Naval family and as a young man made two warship voyages with his grandfather Commodore Samuel Barron. While at the College of William and Mary he was wounded in a duel with pistols. He served the Confederacy and after the war was a prominent lawyer and journalist in Norfolk. He was frequently the poet of choice for Virginia ceremonial occasions. His verse appears also in volumes 3 and 4 of *The Land They Loved*.

The Oath of Freedom

"Liberty is always won where there exists the
unconquerable will to be free."

Born free, thus we resolve to live:

By Heaven we will be free!

By all the stars which burn on high—

By the green earth—the mighty sea—

By God's unshaken majesty,

We will be free or die!

Then let the drums all roll!

Let all the trumpets blow!

Mind, heart, and soul,

We spurn control

Attempted by a foe!

Born free, thus we resolve to live:

By Heaven we will be free!

And, vainly now the Northmen try

To beat us down—in arms we stand

To strike for this our native land!
We will be free or die!

Then let the drums all roll!
Let all the trumpets blow!
Mind, heart, and soul,
We spurn control
Attempted by a foe!

Born free, we thus resolve to live:
By Heaven we will be free!
Our wives and children look on high,
Pray God to smile upon the right!
And bid us in the deadly fight
As freemen live or die!

Then let the drums all roll!
Let all the trumpets blow!
Mind, heart, and soul,
We spurn control
Attempted by a foe!

Born free, thus we resolve to live:
By Heaven we will be free!
And ere we cease this battle-cry,
Be all our blood, our kindred's spilt,
On bayonet or sabre hilt!
We will be free or die!

> Then let the drums all roll!
> Let all the trumpets blow!
> Mind, heart, and soul,
> We spurn control
> Attempted by a foe!

Born free, thus we resolve to live:
By Heaven we will be free!
Defiant let the banners fly,
Shake out their glories to the air,
And, kneeling, brothers, let us swear
We will be free or die!

> Then let the drums all roll!
> Let all the trumpets blow!
> Mind, heart, and soul,
> We spurn control
> Attempted by a foe!

Born free, thus we resolve to live:
By Heaven we will be free!
And to this oath the dead reply—
Our valiant fathers' sacred ghosts—
These with us, and the God of hosts,
We will be free or die!

Then let the drums all roll!
Let all the trumpets blow!
Mind, heart, and soul,
We spurn control
Attempted by a foe!

♦ ♦ ♦

"THE BLESSED UNION." This poet has not been identified.

The Blessed Union

Doubtless to some, with length of ears,
To gratify an ape's desire,
The blessed Union still endears;—
 The stripes, if not the stars, be theirs!
"Greek faith" they gave us eighty years,
And then—"Greek fire!"
But, better all their fires of scaith
Than one hour's trust in Yankee faith!

♦ ♦ ♦

JOHN KILLUM. It is not clear whether this poet has used his real name or a pseudonym.

Old Betsy

Come, with the rifle so long in your keeping,
Clean the old gun up and hurry it forth;
Better to die while "Old Betsy" is speaking,
Than live with arms folded, the slave of the North.
Hear ye the yelp of the North—wolf resounding,
Scenting the blood of the warm-hearted South;
Quick! or his villainous feet will be bounding
Where the gore of our maidens may drip from his mouth.
Oft in the wildwood "Old Bess" has relieved you,
When the fierce bear was cut down in his track—
If at that moment she never deceived you,
Trust her to-day with this ravenous pack.
Then come with the rifle so long in your keeping,
Clean the old girl up and hurry her forth;
Better to die while "Old Betsy" is speaking,
Than live with arms folded, the slave of the North.

◆ ◆ ◆

UNKNOWN AUTHOR from *Prayers Suitable for the Times in Which We Live* published anonymously in Charleston in 1861.

A Prayer for Our Enemies

O God, we beseech Thee, forgive and pardon our enemies, and give us that measure of Thy grace, that for their hatred we may Love them; for their cursing we may bless them; for their injury we may do them good; and for their persecution we may pray for them.

They have laid a net for our steps, and they have digged a pit before us; Lord, we desire not that they themselves should fall into the midst of these, but we beseech Thee keep us out of them, and deliver, establish, bless and prosper us for Thy mercy's sake in Jesus Christ our Saviour, to whom with Thee and the Holy Spirit, we desire to consecrate ourselves and our country, now and forever, imploring Thee to be our GOD, and to make us Thy people.

Amen.

◆ ◆ ◆

II. Poets for the Duration

MARY BAYARD DEVEREUX CLARKE (1827—1886) of North Carolina, was educated at home by her father, a Yale graduate. She was able to travel widely and began writing early. Her first book was *Wood-Notes* (1854), after which she contributed poems prolifically to American and European periodicals. She was gifted in languages and did much translation from European poets, including Victor Hugo's verse. Her plainspoken and down-to-earth writing has often been noted.   (One item below is a humorous treatment of the Yankee invaders' pervasive practice of stealing from civilians.) Her husband was William J. Clarke, a gallant officer in the Mexican War, judge, railroad president, and colonel of the 24th North Carolina Regiment, CSA. They were introduced and married by her uncle Leonidas Polk. Col. Clarke's health was destroyed by a Yankee prison and their later years were difficult. Her comments from a publication of her family papers, *Live Your Own Life*, are often quoted by historians. She continued after the war to be a prolific poet on Christian faith and other themes, and her work will appear again in a later volumes of this series.

The Rebel Sock

In all the pomp and pride of war

The Lincolnite was drest,

High beat his patriotic heart

Beneath his armor'd vest.

His maiden sword hung by his side,

His pistols both were right,

The shining spurs were on his heels,

His coat was buttoned tight.

A firm resolve sat on his brow,

For he to danger went;

By Seward's self that day he was

On secret service sent.

"Mount and away," he sternly cried,
Unto the gallant band,
Who, all equipped from head to heel,
Awaited his command;
"But halt, my boys—before you go,
These solemn words I'll say,
Lincoln expects that every man
His duty'll do to-day."
"We will, we will," the soldiers cried,
"The President shall see,
That we will only run away
From Jackson or from Lee."
And now they're off, just four-score men,
A picked and chosen troop,
And like a hawk upon a dove,
On Maryland they swoop.
From right to left—from house to house,
The little army rides;
In every lady's wardrobe look
To see what there she hides.
They peep in closets, trunks, and drawers,
Examine every box;
Not rebel soldiers now they seek,
But rebel soldiers' socks!
But all in vain!—too keen for them,
Were those dear ladies there,
And not a sock, or flannel shirt
Was taken anywhere.
The day wore on to afternoon,

That warm and drowsy hour,
When Nature's self doth seem to feel
A touch of Morpheus' power;
A farm-house door stood open wide,
The men were all away,
The ladies sleeping in their rooms,
The children at their play;
The house-dog lay upon the step,
But never raised his head,
Though crackling on the gravel walk,
He heard a stranger's trend.
Old grandma, in her rocking chair,
Sat knitting in the hall,
When suddenly upon her work
A shadow seemed to fall.
She raised her eyes and there she saw
Our Federal hero stand,
His little cap was on his head,
His sword was in his hand.
Slowly the dear old lady rose,
And tottering, forward came,
And peering dimly through her "specs,"
Said, "Honey! What's your name?"
Then, as she raised her withered hand,
To pat his sturdy arm,
"There's no one here but Grandmama
And she won't do you harm.
Come, take a seat, and don't be scared,
Put up your sword, my child,

I would not hurt you for the world,"
She gently said, and smiled.
"Madam, my duty must be done
 And I am firm as rock,"
Then, pointing to her work, he said,
"Is that a rebel sock?"
"Yes, Honey, I am getting old
And for hard work ain't fit,
Though for Confederate soldiers,
still, I thank the Lord, can knit."
"Madam, your work is contraband
And Congress confiscates
This rebel sock, which I now seize,
To the United States."
"Yes, Honey—don't be scared—you see
I'll give it up to you."
Then slowly from her half-knit sock
The dame her needles drew,
Broke off the thread, wound up the ball,
And stuck her needles in;
"Here—take it, child—and I to-night
Another will begin."
The soldier next his loyal heart
The dear-bought trophy laid,
And that was all that Seward got
By this old woman's raid.

◆

His Last Word

A few moments before Stonewall Jacksons Death, a sweet smile overspread his face, and he murmured quietly, with an air of relief: 'Let us cross the river and rest under the shade of the trees'.

COME, let us cross the river, and rest beneath the trees,

And list the merry leaflets at sport with every breeze;

Our rest is won by fighting, and Peace awaits us there.

Strange that a cause so blighting produces fruit so fair!

Come, let us cross the river, those that have gone before,

Crush'd in the strife for freedom, await on yonder shore;

So bright the sunshine sparkles, so merry hums the breeze,

Come, let us cross the river, and rest beneath the trees.

Come, let us cross the river, the stream that runs so dark:

'Tis none but cowards quiver, so let us all embark.

Come, men with hearts undaunted, we'll stem the tide with ease,

We'll cross the flowing river, and rest beneath the trees.

Come, let us cross the river, the dying hero cried,

 And God, of life the giver, then bore him o'er the tide.

Life's wars for him are over, the warrior takes his ease,

There, by the flowing river, at rest beneath the trees.

♦

General Lee at The Battle of The Wilderness

There he stood, the grand old hero, great Virginia's god-like son—
Second unto none in glory, equal of her Washington!—
Gazing on his line of battle as it wavered to and fro,
'Neath the front and flank advances of the almost conquering foe;
Calm as was that clear May morning ere the furious death roar broke
From the iron-throated war-lions crouching 'neath their clouds of smoke;
Cool as though the battle raging was but mimicry of fight,
Each brigade an ivory castle and each regiment a knight.
Chafing in reserve beside him two brigades of Texans lay,
All impatient for their portion in the fortune of the day.
Shot and shell are 'mong them falling, yet unmoved they silent stand,
Longing—eager for the battle, but awaiting his command.
Suddenly he rode before them as the forward line gave way,
Raised his hat with courtly gesture—"Follow me and save the day."
But as though by terror stricken, still and silent stood the troop
Who were wont to rush to battle with a fierce avenging whoop;
It was but a single moment, then a murmur through them ran,
Heard above the cannon's roaring as it passed from man to man,
"You go back and we'll go forward," now the waiting leader hears,
Mixed with deep impatient sobbing as of strong men moved to tears,
Once again he gave the order, "I will lead you on the foe";
Then through all their line of battle rang a loud determined "No!"
Quick as thought a gallant major, with a firm and vice—like grasp,
Seized the general's bridle, shouting, "Forward boys, I'll hold him fast."
Then again the hat was lifted, "Sir, I am the older man,

Loose my bridle, I will lead them," in a measured tone and calm.
Trembling with suppressed emotion, with intense excitement hot,
In a quivering voice the Texan, "You shall not, sir, you shall not!"
By them swept the charging squadron with a loud exultant cheer,
"We'll retake the salient, general, if you'll watch us from the rear."
And they kept their word right nobly, sweeping every foe away,
With that grand gray head uncovered watching how they saved the day.
But the god-like calm was shaken, which the battle could not move,
By this true spontaneous token of his soldiers' child-like love.

♦ ♦ ♦

JANE TANDY CROSS (1817—1870) of Kentucky and South Carolina. Regrettably the works of this fine writer have never been collected or fully assessed. Married to a Methodist minister, Dr. Joseph Cross, she lived at times in various States and in Europe. She contributed both verse and prose to journals from a very early age, was fluent in Romance languages, wrote children's stories, and was regarded as an excellent teacher. She and her daughters were imprisoned by the Yankees for six months at Camp Chase, Ohio, for the crime of waving to Confederate raiders passing through Kentucky. Some of her diary has been put on television in a series called "Learned Ladies."

Over the River

We hail your "stripes" and lessened "stars,"

As one may hail a neighbor;

Now forward move! no fear of jars,

With nothing but free labour;

And we will mind our slaves and farm,

And never wish you any harm,

But greet you—over the river.

The self-same language do we speak,

The same dear words we utter;

Then let's not make each other weak,

Nor 'gainst each other mutter;

But let each go his separate way,

And each will doff his hat, and say:

"I greet you—over the river!"

Our flags, almost the same, unfurl,

And nod across the border;

Ohio's waves between them curl—

Our stripe's a little broader;
May yours float out on every breeze,
And, in our wake, traverse all seas—
We greet you—over the river!
We part, as friends of years should part,
With pleasant words and wishes,
And no desire is in our heart
For Lincoln's loaves and fishes;
"Farewell," we wave you from afar,
We like you best—just where you are—
And greet you—over the river!

Nashville *Christian Advocate*, 1861

♦

The Confederacy

Born in a day, full-grown, our Nation stood,
The pearly light of heaven was on her face
Life's early joy was coursing in her blood;
A thing she was of beauty and of grace.

She stood, a stranger on the great broad earth,
No voice of sympathy was heard to greet
The glory-beaming morning of her birth,
Or hail the coming of the unsoiled feet.

She stood, derided by her passing foes;
Her heart beat calmly 'neath their look of scorn;
Their rage in blackening billows round her rose—
Her brow, meanwhile, as radiant as the morn.

Their poisonous coils about her limbs are cast,
She shakes them off in pure and holy ire,
As quietly as Paul, in ages past,
Shook off the serpent in the crackling fire.

She bends not to her foes, nor to the world,
She bears a heart for glory, or for gloom;
But with her starry cross, her flag unfurled,
She kneels amid the sweet magnolia bloom.

She kneels to Thee, O God, she claims her birth,
She lifts to Thee her young and trusting eye,
She asks of Thee her place upon the earth—
For it is Thine to give or to deny.

Oh, let Thine eye but recognize her right!
Oh, let Thy voice but justify her claim!
Like grasshoppers are nations in Thy sight,
And all their power is but an empty name,

Then listen, Father, Listen to her prayer!
Her robes are dripping with her children's blood;
Her foes around "like bulls of Bashan stare,"
They fain would sweep her off, "as with a flood."

The anguish wraps her close around, like death,
Her children lie in heaps about her slain;
Before the world she bravely holds her breath,
Nor gives one utterance to a note of pain.

But 'tis not like Thee to forget the oppressed,
Thou feel'st within her heart the stifled moan—
Thou Christ! Thou Lamb of God! oh, give her rest!
For thou hast called her!—is she not Thine own?

◆

President Davis

The cell is lonely, and the night
Has filled it with a darker gloom;
The little rays of friendly light,
Which through each crack and chink found room
To press in with their noiseless feet,
All merciful and fleet,
And bring, like Noah's trembling dove,
God's silent messages of love—
These, too, are gone, shut out and gone,
And that great heart is left alone.

Alone, with darkness and with woe,
Around him Freedom's temple lies,
Its arches crushed, its columns low,
The night-wind through its ruin sighs,
Rash, cruel hands that temple razed,
Then stood the world amazed!
And now those hands—ah, ruthless deeds!
Their captive pierce—his brave heart bleeds;
And yet no groan
Is heard, no groan!
He suffers silently, alone.

For all his bright and happy home,
He has that cell, so drear and dark,

The narrow walls, for heaven's blue dome,
The clank of chains, for song of lark;
And for the grateful voice of friends—
That voice which ever lends
Its charm where human hearts are found—
He hears the key's dull, grating sound;
No heart is near,
No kind heart near,
No sigh of sympathy, no tear!

Oh, dream not thus, though true and good!
Unnumbered hearts on thee await,
By thee invisibly have stood,
Have crowded through thy prison-gate;
Nor dungeon bolts, nor dungeon bars,
Nor floating "stripes and stars,"
Nor glittering gun or bayonet,
Can ever cause us to forget
Our faith to thee,
Our love to thee,
Thou glourious soul! thou strong! thou free!

(To President Davis in Prison.)

◆ ◆ ◆

COLUMBUS DREW (1820—1891) was born in Washington D.C. to English immigrant parents. He was an active journalist in antebellum Washington when he was encouraged to move to Florida and establish a newspaper in Jacksonville. Much of his Confederate verse celebrates the extraordinary deeds of Col. John Jackson Dickison and his small group of Florida men who defeated the Union Army every time it tried to move from the seaports. Drew was appointed Comptroller in the redeemed state government at the end of Reconstruction. He continued to be a prolific poet and his work will appear in later volumes of this series.

Uncle Sam

Old Sam is dead—old Uncle Sam—
Old Uncle Sam-u-el!
The briny tears fall from my head
Whene'er his name I tell.

He used to wear a long blue coat,
With buttons down before,
A standing collar round his throat,
With lace bedizzened o'er

And on those buttons—I must not
Forget it—no I can't—
The good old bird of Liberty
Was gloriously rampant.

He used to wear a big chapeau
When out on full parade,
A massive plume of drifted snow,
With crimson top displayed.

A ponderous scabbard by his side,
And sword of steel so bright,
And high-top boots of mighty stride,
Equipped him for the fight.

He used to brag about a rag
He loved to see outspread,
Nor strife nor storm e'er shook his form,
With that above his head.

The stars and stripes his spirit kissed
As some potential charm,
Born of the rainbow's tri-hued mist
To shield his land from harm.

His civic coat was swallow-tail
Low reaching in its frisk,
With buttons twain though brassy plain,
Of most capacious disk.

This was the rear view—in the fore
His gaudy striped vest
And trousers, still redeemed from yore
The gules upon his crest.

His hat (ah, that was nigh forgot),
Was bell-crown to a tee,
And then instead of sheath or blade
A chain and seal wore he.

Of course where army boots were put
Aside for dress, perhaps
You'll know without my telling you
His pants were held with "straps."

And this was UNCLE SAM of State,
'Twas thus his title ran
His simple civic soubriquet was
BROTHER JONATHAN!

And he is dead—that good old man?
And shall we see no more
His bell-crown hat, or nodding plume,
Or buttons down before?

Or is he only in a trance,
That binds him in his prime,
The while his "sovereign" urchins "dance,"
And have a jolly time.

He must be gone! but yet his ghost
Still lingers where he fought,
And seems to have a hankering
For what his money bought.

(Jacksonville, March 13, 1861)

◆

The Grey-Clad Partisan

The camp was down at Waldo—the soldiers numbered more,

Within its rude-built houses, than five full valiant score

It was a Spartan city, embowered among the pines,

And men grew strong on frugal fare within its tented lines.

'Twas oft for days deserted, save by the guard, whose feet,

Now that a lion watched the path, all careless trod his beat,

For Dickison was scouting, and once upon the track,

Well had the sentry learned to wait till triumph brought him back.

And true as comes the needle, long vibrating, to its place,

Came the leader back to Waldo, from his hundredth warpath chase,

And the fires of camp were lighted, and the harness of the field

Was loosed from weary limbs, and hung, as ancients hung the shield,

And the groups were scattered gaily where the scanty board was
    spread,

With the cup of cool spring water, and the bacon and the bread,

And the pipes were wreathing garlands for the gentle zephyr wave.

As love exhales its garlands round the gentle and the brave,

Here one with tale of war beguiled the night's slow-waning hours,

And saw in dreams the look that smiled from Love's o'ershadowing
    bowers,

There one sweet song's enchanting spell breathed fondly o'er the scene,

And tuned the lay of hope to meet the maid of Augustine

Thus sang the valiant soldier boy, his face illumed, that night,

With his soul's flash, that rose to join the flickering camp-fire light.

♦

Camp Song of the St. Augustine Confederate

I

I soon may see, no more to part,
The maid who waits her lover—
Who waits until, with trusting heart,
This cruel war is over.
She dwells in dear St. Augustine,
Her hair is black and braided—
She bade me go and stand to guard
Our sunny soil invaded.

I soon may see my loved brunette,
By San Sebastian, flowing—
Perchance her watching eyes are wet,
Or brave and hopeful glowing
I soon may meet those deep dark eyes—
May meet that heart, ne'er doubting,
Save when she hears the quick surprise,
Or lists the mingled shouting.

For when our "Eagle" swoops around,
And rifle—notes are ringing,
That heart, all still to catch the sound,
More close to mine is clinging,
I'll clasp it yet—I'll clasp it true—
That heart so bravely beating,
That bids me dare and bids me do,
And nobly win the meeting.

The camp at Waldo slumbered, for the hundreth warpath raid
Had led them—sweet betrayal—to the dreamer's ambuscade.

II

'Twas night again at Waldo, and the men were all alert,
And Dickison girded well his sword upon his skirt.
A rumor vague was passing, by none well understood,
Save by the valiant leader, the Pine Grove Robin Hood.
The hero band of Waldo were destined now to do
 Some duty full of peril, but of fear not to the true,
And ready to the summons, each rider was on horse,
And marching with his leader on his early morning course
Through the deep sandy highway, through the cool hammock glade,
While the great sun rolled westward, east marched the cavalcade,
And as the night fell on them, paused they at last to bait
Rider and beast a moment, there at the peril gate
One league 'twas from Palatka, this place of bivouac
An hour, and none that starteth can, craven-like, turn back,
For once upon the river, the beautiful St. John,
Their safety lay in finishing the work they'd set upon.
By a few torches gleaming, the leader called his men,
Up in a line before him reined they their coursers then—
Each with a day's provision, a corn-blade sheaf well tied
Upon the saddle rearward, with holsters at the side.
Thus mounted well and ready, the torches' fitful gleam,
Made some romantic picture the peril—hunters seem
The "great rebellion's" Marion, to lead a captain born,
With his own hand his steed attired, and took his sheaf of corn.

His trusty sword well girded, his weapons all aprime,
He sprang into his saddle like a knight of olden time,
Then, when the steeds were chafing, and fronted in the light,
"Men!" said the valiant Dickison, "we cross the stream to-night;
Be silent going over—'tis danger we must meet,
To the eastward of the river that opposes our retreat;
For when ourselves and friendship it rolls its waves between,
The foe may overwhelm us from the walls of Augustine
We go again to thwart him, to harass and to strike,
To beard him in his stronghold as the surf upon the dyke—
If one be for the journey unwilling or o'erworn,
Let him go back to Waldo with the wagons in the morn."
He waited then in silence, but no faltering voice was heard
"March!" and the boys of Dickison were moving at the word.

III

Five score of hardy yeomen, though quiet was their tread,
Wakened Palatka, desolate as city of the dead.
There in its lone deserted streets the chargers and the men
Waited the scanty transport o'er, in couples ten by ten.
The oarsmen well were chosen, and labored through the night
Where lurked upon the river the peril of the fight.
The morn broke bright upon them, and still, upon the tide,
'Twas noon before the rowers' last firm oar had plied.
Strange chance, the band, in crossing by decimal relief,
The foe had not discovered and brought to speedy grief!
But there they stood together, upon the hostile shore,

Each rider in his saddle, and away a moment more—
Away for Picolata, like Cossacks of the Don,
To spy or strike the barbican that frowned on the St. John.
From wary reconnoitre, before the dawn had broke,
The scouts report the battlements would laugh to meet the stroke.
Transplanted were the forest pines in strong compacted square,
Safe shielding thrice the riflemen who came to charge them there:
Such the report the scouts received, false-witnessed, but availed
To save a feeble garrison, fated if then assailed.
The leader turned, well-purposed not to sacrifice the few,
In many a 'vironed peril-path had proved him doubly true,
"Come as the wind, my men," he spoke, "it reeks not where we fall,
Whether on roving predators or badly guarded wall,
Swift be our work—the odds are theirs—we have no doubt to choose,
We take the hostile eastward paths to win and not to lose."

♦

The Last Look of the Dying Soldier

'Twas the last look he gave when left dying alone,
All his cherished companions now prostrate and gone
Still conscious he lay on the field where he fell,
And his eyes gave response to his bosom's "All's well"
For only a true heart in death says all's well.

He had left a fond home untutored in fight,
For before war's red banner ne'er greeted his sight,
And the tear of the mother that fell on his brow
Had not, in its love, seemed to burn until now,
'Mid the death-dew that chilled it, that tear burned it now.

When the fallen in battle all silently lay,
The eye saw the light of the calm summer's day,
As one bids adieu to some loved, fading shore,
The sight that then blessed him should bless him no more.
That look was the last on life's fading shore.

Though dim grew his eye, still the picture was grand—
The battle of life on the long-reaching strand,
And far in the rear from its peril away,
The cot of his childhood so peacefully lay,
He fancied himself on its threshold at play.

A moment though thick o'er his eyes came the haze,
His look at the cot met the mother's fond gaze

That look as the vision so silently passed—
Contented but mournful—that look was the last;
The look of the soldier, the dying, the last.

He lifted his hand as the eyelids were sealed,
As awed by a glimpse to the spirit revealed,
And quickly it fell on his bosom at rest—
That bosom his mother, ah! fain would have pressed—
It fell on the Bible he wore 'neath his vest.

She gave it at parting, and bade him to keep
That book on his bosom, awake or in sleep,
And oft on its pages, as hardships he passed,
When waking or weary, a love look he cast,
And blest was the look of the soldier, the last.

(Lake City, December 21, 1862)

♦

All Quiet Upon The Olustee To-Night

"I visited the field of Olustee. The dead were all buried as soon as possible after the battle, but when I beheld the place, amid the solitude of the towering pines, the owl was hooting its dismal monody, and the pits or graves wherein the dead were placed, had been uncovered either by swine or vultures, and the bones of many of the dead were scattered around. I noticed an arm torn from the body, and still in the sleeve of a Confederate jacket. The scene was one of the sad commentaries upon war." –Newspaper Correspondent

All quiet upon the Olustee to-night—

For a scout from his round is returning,

And tells how his heart sadly mused at the sight,

Though late in its triumph 'twas burning.

"All quiet the field of Olustee I saw,

While dimly the stars shone upon it,

But ah! 'twas a triumph that mingles with awe

The pride that still whispers 'We won it!'

Ah! quiet indeed is Olustee to-night!"

We buried the dead on the field where they fell,

The pines were the plumes that hung o'er them,

And wafted, with every depression and swell,

The Death-Angel's wing—shade before them.

'Twas something that spoke to the clamor "Be still!"

And hushed was the din at the fiat—

The angel of Battle, subdued by the will

Of Death, left Olustee all quiet—

All quiet upon the Olustee that night!

The moonlight fell faint on the field of the air
Through quick-moving cloud-rifts diffusing,
And fought with the star-light for mastery there,
That night when the lone scout was musing.
But ah! by the light he could see the torn shroud—
The earth-shroud the soldier encumbered—
And bones of the forms that in quiet had bowed,
 All scattered, unknown and unnumbered
 All quiet and dead on Olustee that night!

The boy from his cottage far down in the pines,
The sire from the mountains fruit-bearing,
The brother, from tending the scuppernong vines,
All nobly to duty repairing,
The shock of Olustee, the battle's sharp blast,
Met firmly, resolved to defy it
And there the lone scout, now the battle is past,
Unites with his comrades in quiet,
A moment upon the Olustee that night.

The breezes still sound through the tall forest pines,
The guards of Olustee, long biding,
Still gurgles its name, as in musical lines,
The stream in the "bay" ever hiding
Still dreams the lone scout, as he checks there his steed,
Perchance for repose, ever jaded,

Of comrades that sleep there—of heroes that bleed,
To shelter our homesteads invaded,
When quiet reigns on the Olustee at night.

All quiet upon the Olustee to-night!
But ah! there are hearts beating quicker,
Far off and far louder than drums in the fight,
Like hosts that in danger grow thicker,
"A mother bereaved or a sister bereft,
Perchance calls some name in her dreaming,"
And clasps some loved form, in a dream only left,
That lies where the starlight is gleaming
All quiet upon the Olustee to-night!

(Lake City, Fla., July 29th, 1864)

♦

Only A Tramp

In a hospital tent a sick soldier was lying,
Wounded and weary and worn;
Physician and chaplain both saw he was dying,
The spark of life soon would be gone

They told him at last that the end was at hand—
That the term of his service was spent—
They asked him his home and the name of a friend,
That a message away might be sent.

He answered them thus, as a smile seemed to roam
O'er his face upon which was death's damp:
"I have not a friend, and my country's my home;
I enlisted though only a tramp."

Out flickered the light and the eyes closed in sleep,
And they folded his hands on his breast,
In the woods by the river, where clinging vines creep,
His comrades they laid him to rest.

Only a tramp. Yet he answered the call
To fight 'neath the flag of the free!
Only a tramp. He hath given his all—
For his country, for you and for me.

When swords we present to the living and brave
Who are yet in the field or the camp,
It is wrong to forget, in his far-away grave,
The boy who was only a tramp.

And when we erect shafts of marble and brass,
And records of valor there stamp,
Shall we add not a word of the grave 'neath the grass,
Of the hero though only a tramp?

♦

Song of The Spinning Wheel

Out of the garret, out of the barn,
Summoned am I to my duty;
Long set aside with my lustreless yarn,
Robbed of my fabric of beauty.
I'm summoned to come with a whir and a hum,
With the voice like the flying of chaff
From some mighty machine that the grain may be clean—
'Tis but me and my mighty distaff.

But, the grain winnowed, the fan of the silk,—
Let fly the satins and laces;
Soldier's array I'll supply to my ilk,
Veils for my daughters' bright faces.
So will I sing with a whir and a hum,
I sing, while now my dear daughters
Have saddest of faces; alas! there are some
Quaff deep of woe's bitter waters.

When I am singing then I work best,
Work, though I know the storm rages;
I'll do my duty and leave all the rest
To patriot soldiers and sages
So with a whiz and a whir and a hum,
E'en in the roughest of weather,
Something in tune with the roll of the drum,
For we are workers together.

◆ ◆ ◆

PAUL HAMILTON HAYNE (1830—1886) of South Carolina was a romantic poet who greatest popularity came after the War, although his verse appears in both the volume preceding and the volume following this one of Confederate poets. The Yankee bombardment of Charleston destroyed his home and library, and he lived thereafter in a cabin in the woods near Augusta, Georgia.

Charleston

WHAT! still does the Mother of Treason uprear
Her crest 'gainst the Furies that darken her sea?
Unquelled by mistrust, and unblanched by a Fear,
Unbowed her proud head, and unbending her knee,
Calm, steadfast, and free?

Aye! launch your red lightnings, blaspheme in your wrath,
Shock earth, wave, and heaven with the blasts of your ire; —
But she seizes your death—bolts, yet hot from their path,
And hurls back your lightnings, and mocks at the fire
Of your fruitless desire.

Ringed round by her Brave, a fierce circlet of flame,
Flashes up from the sword—points that cover her breast
She is guarded by Love, and enhaloed by Fame,
And never, we swear, shall your footsteps be pressed
Where her dead heroes rest!

Her voice shook the Tyrant—sublime from her tongue
Fell the accents of warning,—a Prophetess grand,—
On her soil the first life-notes of Liberty rung,
And the first stalwart blow of her gauntleted hand
Broke the sleep of her land!

What more! she hath grasped with her iron-bound will
The Fate that would trample her honour to earth,—
The light in those deep eyes is luminous still
With the warmth of her valor, the glow of her worth,
Which illumine the Earth!

And beside her a Knight the great Bayard had loved,
"Without fear or reproach," lifts her Banner on high;
He stands in the vanguard, majestic unmoved,
And a thousand firm souls, when that Chieftain is nigh
Vow, "'tis easy to die!"

Their swords have gone forth on the fetterless air!
The world's breath is hushed at the conflict! before
Gleams the bright form of Freedom with wreaths in
     her hair—
And what though the chaplet be crimsoned with gore,
We shall prize her the more!

And while Freedom lures on with her passionate eyes
To the height of her promise, the voices of yore,
From the storied Profound of past ages arise,
And the pomps of their magical music outpour
O'er the war—beaten shore.

Then gird your brave Empress, O! Heroes, with flame
Flashed up from the sword—points that cover her breast.
She is guarded by Love, and enhaloed by Fame,
And never, base Foe! shall your footsteps be pressed
Where her dead Martyrs rest!

◆

Vicksburg — A Ballad

For sixty days and upwards,
A storm of shell and shot
Rained round us in a flaming shower,
But still we faltered not.
"If the noble city perish,"
Our grand young leader said,
"Let the only walls the foe shall scale
Be ramparts of the dead!"

For sixty days and upwards,
The eye of heaven waxed dim;
And e'en throughout God's holy morn,
O'er Christian prayer and hymn,
Arose a hissing tumult,
As if the fiends in air
Strove to engulf the voice of faith
In the shrieks of their despair.

There was wailing in the houses,
There was trembling on the marts,
While the tempest raged and thundered,
'Mid the silent thrill of hearts;
But the Lord, our shield, was with us,
And ere a month had sped,
Our very women walked the streets
With scarce one throb of dread.

And the little children gambolled,
Their faces purely raised,
Just for a wondering moment,
As the huge bombs whirled and blazed,
Then turned with silvery laughter
To the sports which children love,
Thrice-mailed in the sweet, instinctive thought
That the good God watched above.

Yet the hailing bolts fell faster,
From scores of flame-clad ships,
And about us, denser, darker,
Grew the conflict's wild eclipse,
Till a solid cloud closed o'er us,
Like a type of doom and ire,
Whence shot a thousand quivering tongues
Of forked and vengeful fire.

But the unseen hands of angels
Those death—shafts warned aside,
And the dove of heavenly mercy
Ruled o'er the battle tide;
In the houses ceased the wailing,
And through the war—scarred marts
The people strode, with step of hope,
To the music in their hearts.

♦

Sonnet

RISE from your gory ashes stern and pale,
Ye martyred thousands! and with dreadful ire,
A voice of doom, a front of gloomy fire,
Rebuke those faithless souls, whose querulous wail
Disturbs your sacred sleep! —"The withering hail
Of battle, hunger, pestilence, despair,
Whatever of mortal anguish man may bear,
We bore unmurmuring! strengthened by the mail
Of a most holy purpose!—then we died!—
Vex not our rest by cries of selfish pain,
But to the noblest measure of your powers
Endure the appointed trial! Griefs defied,
But launch their threatening thunderbolts in vain,
And angry storms pass by in gentlest showers!"

♦

Addressed to Henry Timrod, Esq.

Bold Minstrel! earnest patriot! who shall say,
Albeit thine arm against our general foe,
In open strife, hath dealt no mortal blow,
Thou hast not borne thee nobly in the fray,
Thy mind's impetuous cohorts, thine array,
Of passionate fancies, feelings grand and high
Have striven where thoughts ethereal fly,
On many a well fought field and glorious day!
The kindling muse hath pealed her clarion song
O'er land and ocean! souls of faltering will
Leap to the stormy music, and are strong—
While the roused pulses of the popular heart
Swayed by the magic of thy conquering skill,
Attest the electric energy of Art!

♦ ♦ ♦

EMILY J. MOORE. This fine poet appears in several postbellum collections of Confederate verse but has not been further identified.

The Salkehatchie

The crystal streams, the pearly streams,
   The streams in sunbeams flashing,
The murm'ring streams, the gentle streams,
   The streams down mountains dashing,
     Have been the theme
     Of poets' dream,
   And, in wild witching story,
Have been renowned for love's fond scenes,
   Or some great deed of glory.

     The Rhine, the Tiber, Ayr, and Tweed,
       The Arno, silver-flowing,
     The Hudson, Charles, Potomac, Don,
       With poesy are glowing;
         But I would praise
         In artless lays,
       A stream which well may match ye,
      Though dark its waters glide along—
       The swampy Salkehatchie.

'Tis not the beauty of its stream,
   Which makes it so deserving
Or honour at the Muses' hands,

But 'tis the use it's serving,
And 'gainst a raid,
We hope its aid
Will ever prove efficient,
Its fords remain still overflowed,
In water ne'er deficient.
If Vandal bands are held in check,
Their crossing thus prevented,
And we are spared the ravage wild
Their malice has invented,
Then we may well
In numbers tell
No other stream can match ye,
And grateful we shall ever be
To swampy Salkehatchie.

♦

Tell The Boys The War Is Ended

(While in the first ward of the Quintard Hospital, Rome, Georgia, a young soldier from the Eighth Arkansas Regiment, who had been wounded at Murfreesboro', called me to his bedside. As I approached I saw that he was dying, and when I bent over him he was just able to whisper, "Tell the boys the war is ended.")

"TELL the boys the war is ended,"
These were all the words he said;
"Tell the boys the war is ended,"
In an instant more was dead.
Strangely bright, serene, and cheerful
Was the smile upon his face,
While the pain, of late so fearful,
Had not left the slightest trace.

"Tell the boys the war is ended,"
And with heavenly visions bright
Thoughts of comrades loved were blended,
As his spirit took its flight.
"Tell the boys the war is ended,"
"Grant, O God, it may be so,"
Was the prayer which then ascended,
In a whisper deep, though low.

"Tell the boys the war is ended,"
And his warfare then was o'er,
As, by angel bands attended,
He departed from earth's shore.
Bursting shells and cannons roaring
Could not rouse him by their din;
He to better worlds was soaring,
Far from war, and pain, and sin.

♦ ♦ ♦

ALBERT PIKE (1809—1891) of Arkansas, though born in Boston, adventured to the frontier as a young man. He served in the Mexican War, as legal counsel to the Five Civilised Tribes, and as a Confederate general. He was already well-known as a poet when he penned these lines as patriotic lyrics for "Dixie."

Dixie to Arms!

(1861)

Southrons, hear ye Country call ye!

Up! Lest worse than death befall you!

    To arms! To arms! To arms! In Dixie!

Lo! All the beacon fires are lighted,

Let all hearts be now united!

    To arms! To arms! To arms! In Dixie!

    Advance the flag of Dixie

       Hurrah! Hurrah!

    For Dixie's land we take our stand,

    To live or die for Dixie!

       To arms! To arms!

    And conquer peace for Dixie!

       To arms! To arms!

    And conquer peace for Dixie!

Oh hear the Northern thunders mutter!

Northern flags in South winds flutter,

    To arms! To arms! To arms! In Dixie!

Send them back your fierce defiance!

Stamp upon the cursed alliance!
    To arms! To arms! To arms! In Dixie!

    Advance the flag of Dixie
      Hurrah! Hurrah!
For Dixie's land we take our stand,
To live or die for Dixie!
    To arms! To arms!
And conquer peace for Dixie!
    To arms! To arms!
And conquer peace for Dixie!

Fear no danger! Shun no labor!
Lift up rifle, pike, and saber!
    To arms! To arms! To arms! In Dixie!
Shoulder press and post to shoulder,
Let the odds make each heart bolder!
    To arms! To arms! To arms! In Dixie!

    Advance the flag of Dixie,
      Hurrah! Hurrah!
For Dixie's land we take our stand,
To live or die for Dixie!
    To arms! To arms!
And conquer peace for Dixie!
    To arms! To arms!
And conquer peace for Dixie!

Then I wish I was in Dixie,
    Hurrah! Hurrah!
For Dixie's land we take our stand,
To live or die in Dixie!
Away, away, away down south in Dixie!
Away, away, away down in Dixie!

♦

The Magnolia

What, what is the true Southern Symbol,
The Symbol of Honour and Right,
The Emblem that suits a brave people
In arms against number and might?
'Tis the ever green stately Magnolia,
Its pearl—flowers pure as the Truth,
Defiant of tempest and lightning,
Its life a perpetual youth.

French blood stained with glory the Lilies,
While centuries marched to their grave;
And over bold Scot and gay Irish
The Thistle and Shamrock yet wave:
Ours, ours be the noble Magnolia,
That only on Southern soil grows
The Symbol of life everlasting:—
Dear to us as to England the Rose.

Paint the flower on a field blue as Heaven,
Let the broad leaves around it be seen,
"Semper virens" the eloquent motto,
Our colors the Blue, White and Green.
Type of Chivalry, loyalty, virtue,
In Winter and Summer the same,
Full of leaf, full of flower, full of vigor—
It befits those who fight for a name.

For a name among Earth's ancient Nations,
Yet more for the Truth and the Right,
For Freedom, for proud Independence,
The old strife of Darkness and Light.
Round the World bear the flag of our glory,
While the nations look on and admire,
And our struggle, immortal in story,
Shall the free of all ages inspire.

What though many fall in the conflict,
And our blood redden many a field?
The foe's on our soil, fellow—soldiers!
And God is our strength and our shield.
Through the fire and the smoke bear our banner
Ever on, while a fragment remains!
What though we are few and they many?
The Lord God of Armies still reigns.

♦ ♦ ♦

MARGARET JUNKIN PRESTON (1820—1897) of Lexington, Virginia, was the sister of Stonewall Jackson's first wife, who died tragically young. In addition to wartime verse, she wrote some of the deepest reflections on Confederate defeat. These will appear in the next volume.

Hymn to The National Flag

Float aloft, thou stainless banner!
Azure cross and field of light;
Be thy brilliant stars the symbol
Of the pure and true and right.
Shelter freedom's holy cause—
Liberty and sacred laws;
Guard the youngest of the nations—
Keep her virgin honour bright

From Virginia's storied border,
Down to Tampa's furthest shore—
From the blue Atlantic's clashings
To the Rio Grande's roar—
Over many a crimson plain,
Where our martyred ones lie slain—
Fling abroad thy blessed shelter,
Stream and mount and valley o'er.

In thy cross of heavenly azure
Has our faith its emblem high;
In thy field of white, the hallow'd

Truth for which we'll dare and die;
In thy red, the patriot blood—
Ah! the consecrated flood.
Lift thyself, resistless banner!
Ever fill our Southern sky!

Flash with living, lightning motion
In the sight of all the brave!
Tell the price at which we purchased
Room and right for thee to wave
Freely in our God's free air,
Pure and proud and stainless fair,
Banner of the youngest nation—
Banner we would die to save!

Strike Thou for us! King of armies!
Grant us room in Thy broad world!
Loosen all the despot's fetters,
Back— be all his legions hurled!
Give us peace and liberty,
Let the land we love be free—
Then, oh! Bright and stainless banner!
Never shall thy folds be furled!

◆

The Shade of The Trees

What are the thoughts that are stirring his breast?
What is the mystical vision he sees?
"Let us pass over the river, and rest
Under the shade of the trees."

Has he grown sick of his toils and his tasks?
Sighs the worn spirit for respite or ease?
Is it a moment's cool halt that he asks
"Under the shade of the trees."

Is it the gurgle of waters whose flow
Ofttime has come to him, borne on the breeze,
Memory listens to, lapsing so low,
Under the shade of the trees?

Nay—though the rasp of the flesh was so sore,
Faith, that had yearnings far keener than these,
Saw the soft sheen of the Thitherward Shore,
Under the shade of the trees;—

Caught the high psalms of ecstatic delight,
Heard the harps harping, like soundings of seas,
Watched earth's assoiled ones, walking in white
Under the shade of the trees.

O, was it strange he should pine for release,
Touched to the soul with such transports as these,
He who so needed the balsam of peace,
Under the shade of the trees?

Yea, it was noblest for him—it was best
(Questioning naught of our Father's decrees)
There to pass over the river and rest
Under the shade of the trees!

(The death of Stonewall Jackson.)

♦

Only A Private

''Only a private;—and who will care
When I may pass away,—
Or how, or why I perish, or where
I mix with the common clay?
They will fill my empty place again
With another as bold and brave;
And they'll blot me out ere the Autumn rain
Has freshened my nameless grave.''

"Only a private;—it matters not
That I did my duty well,
That all through a score of battles I fought,
And then, like a soldier, fell:
The country I died for—never will heed
My unrequited claim;
And history cannot record the deed,
For she never has heard my name.''

"Only a private;—and yet I know,
When I heard the rallying call,
I was one of the very first to go,
And ... I'm one of the many who fall:
But, as here I lie, it is sweet to feel,
That my honour's without a stain—
That I only fought for my Country's weal,
And not for glory or gain.''

"Only a private;—yet He who reads
Through the guises of the heart,
Looks not at the splendor of the deeds,
But the way we do our part;
And when He shall take us by the hand,
And our small service own,
There'll a glorious band of privates stand
As victors around the throne!"

The breath of the morning is heavy and chill,
And gloomily lower the mists on the hill;
The winds through the beeches are shivering low,
With a plaintive and sad miserere of woe:
A quiet is over the Cottage—a dread
Clouds the children's sweet faces—Macpherson is dead!

◆ ◆ ◆

JAMES RYDER RANDALL (1839–1908) was a Maryland native who had, like so many other Southerners, moved west, to Louisiana. He wrote this first poem at the very beginning of The War in hope that Maryland would be able to follow Virginia into the Confederacy. Unfortunately, Lincoln's military coup d'etat prevented Marylanders from making a free decision. Where their allegiance lay is indicated by the number of Marylanders who volunteered for the Confederate Army, and by the fact that "Maryland, My Maryland" was adopted as the official State song after the U. S. Army left. The verses are sung to the familiar tune of "Tannenbaum."

Maryland, My Maryland

The despot's heel is on thy shore,

 Maryland!

His torch is at thy temple door

 Maryland!

Avenge the patriotic gore

That flecked the streets of Baltimore,

And be the battle—queen of yore,

 Maryland, my Maryland!

Hark to an exiled son's appeal,

 Maryland!

My Mother State, to thee I kneel,

 Maryland!

For life and death, for woe and weal,

Thy peerless chivalry reveal,

And gird thy beauteous limbs with steel,

 Maryland, my Maryland!

Thou wilt not cower in the dust,
    Maryland!
Thy beaming sword shall never rust,
    Maryland!
Remember Carroll's sacred trust,
Remember Howard's warlike thrust,
And all thy slumberers with the just,
    Maryland, my Maryland!

Come! 'tis the red dawn of the day,
    Maryland!
Come with thy panoplied array,
    Maryland!
With Ringgold's spirit for the fray,
With Watson's blood at Monterey,
With fearless Lowe and dashing May,
    Maryland, my Maryland!

Come! for thy shield is bright and strong,
    Maryland!
Come! for thy dalliance does thee wrong,
    Maryland!
Come to thine own heroic throng,
Stalking with Liberty along,
And chant thy dauntless slogan—song,
    Maryland, my Maryland!

Dear Mother, burst the tyrant's chain,
      Maryland!
Virginia should not call in vain,
      Maryland!
She meets her sisters on the plain,—
"Sic semper!" 'tis the proud refrain
That baffles minions back amain,
      Maryland, my Maryland!

I see the blush upon thy cheek,
      Maryland!
For thou wast ever bravely meek,
      Maryland!
But lo! there surges forth a shriek
From hill to hill, from creek to creek,—
Potomac calls to Chesapeake,
      Maryland, my Maryland!

Thou wilt not yield the Vandal toll,
      Maryland!
Thou wilt not crook to this control,
      Maryland!
Better the fire upon thee roll,
Better the blade, the shot, the bowl,
Than crucifixion of the soul,
      Maryland, my Maryland!

I hear the distant thunder—hum,
    Maryland!
The Old Line's bugle, fife, and drum,
She is not dead, nor deaf, nor dumb;
Huzza! She spurns the Northern scum!
She breathes! she burns! she'll come!
She'll come!
    Maryland, my Maryland!

◆

John Pelham

Just as the spring came laughing through the strife
With all its gorgeous cheer;
In the bright April of historic life
Fell the great cannoneer.

The wondrous lulling of a hero's breath
His bleeding country weeps—
Hushed in the alabaster arms of death,
Our young Marcellus sleeps.

Nobler and grander than the Child of Rome,
Curbing his chariot steeds;
The knightly scion of a Southern home
Dazzled the land with deeds.

Gentlest and bravest in the battle brunt,
The champion of the truth,
He bore his banner to the very front
Of our immortal youth.

A clang of sabres 'mid Virginia snow,
The fiery rush of shells—
And there's a wail of immemorial woe
In Alabama dells.

The pennon drops that led the sabered band
Along the crimson field!
The meteor blade sinks from the nerveless hand
Over the spotless shield.

We gazed and gazed upon that beauteous face,
While 'round the lips and eyes,
Couched in the marble slumber, flashed the grace
Of a divine surprise.

Oh, Mother of a blessed soul on high!
Thy tears may soon be shed—
Think of thy boy with princes of the sky,
Among the Southern dead.

How must he smile on this dull world beneath,
Fevered with swift renown—
He—with the martyr's amaranthine wreath
Twining the victor's crown!

March 17, 1863

♦

At Fort Pillow

You shudder as you think upon
The carnage of the grim report,
The desolation when we won
The inner trenches of the fort.

But there are deeds you may not know,
That scourge the pulses into strife;
Dark memories of deathless woe
Pointing the bayonet and knife.

The house is ashes where I dwelt,
Beyond the mighty inland sea;
The tombstones shattered where I knelt,
By that old Church in Pointe Coupée.

The Yankee fiends that came with fire,
Camped on the consecrated sod,
And trampled in the dust and mire
The Holy Eucharist of God!

The spot where darling mother sleeps,
Beneath the glimpse of yon sad moon,
Is crushed, with splintered marble heaps,
To stall the horse of some dragoon!

God! when I ponder that black day,
It makes my frantic spirit wince;
I marched—with Longstreet—far away,
But have beheld the ravage since.

The tears are hot upon my face
When thinking what bleak fate befell
The only sister of our race—
A thing too horrible to tell.

They say that, ere her senses fled,
She rescue of her brothers cried;
Then feebly bowed her stricken head,
Too pure to live thus—so she died.

Two of those brothers heard no plea
With their proud hearts forever still—
John shrouded by the Tennessee,
And Arthur there at Malvern Hill.

But I have heard it everywhere,
Vibrating like a passing knell;
'Tis as perpetual as the air,
And solemn as a funeral bell.

By scorched lagoon and murky swamp
My wrath was never in the lurch;

I've killed the picket in his camp,
And many a pilot on his perch.

With steady rifle, sharpened brand,
A week ago, upon my steed,
With Forrest and his warrior band,
I made the hell-hounds writhe and bleed.

You should have seen our leader go
Upon the battle's burning marge,
Swooping like falcon, on the foe,
Heading the gray line's iron charge!

All outcasts from our ruined marts,
We heard th' undying serpent hiss,
And in the desert of our hearts
The fatal spell of Nemesis.

The Southern yell rang loud and high
The moment that we thundered in,
Smiting the demons hip and thigh,
Cleaving them to the very chin.

My right arm bared for fiercer play,
The left one held the rein in slack;
In all the fury of the fray
I sought the white man, not the black.

The dabbled clots of brain and gore
Across the swirling sabres ran;
To me each brutal visage bore
The front of one accursed man.

Throbbing along the frenzied vein,
My blood seemed kindled into song—
The death-dirge of the sacred slain,
The slogan of immortal wrong.

It glared athwart the dripping glaves,
It blazed in each avenging eye—
The thought of desecrated graves,
And some lone sister's desperate cry!

♦ ♦ ♦

WILLIAM GILMORE SIMMS (1806—1870) of South Carolina, amazingly prolific novelist, poet, essayist, lecturer, historian, critic, and editor, has been rightly called "The Father of Southern Literature." Without question Simms is the most important Southern writer of the 19th century after Poe. Without question Simms is in every way one of the most important American writers. It is a scandal that Boston and New York critics have left him out of the canon. As a major American writer and a South Carolinian, Simms lived The War. This section includes perhaps a fourth or so of Simms's war poetry. Many items were published unsigned, but Simms's authorship has been verified by Prof. James E. Kibler.

The Irrepressible Conflict

THEN welcome be it, if indeed it be

The Irrepressible Conflict! Let it come;

There will be mitigation of the doom,

If, battling to the last, our sires shall see

Their sons contending for the homes made free

In ancient conflict with the foreign foe!

If those who call us brethren strike the blow,

No common conflict shall the invader know!

War to the knife, and to the last, until

The sacred land we keep shall overflow

With blood as sacred—valley, wave, and hill,

 Or the last enemy finds his bloody grave!

Aye, welcome to your graves—or ours!

The brave May perish, but ye shall not bind one slave.

♦

Sonnet

Democracy hath done its work of ill,
And, seeming freemen, never to be free,
While the poor people shout in vanity,
The Demagogue triumphs o'er the popular will.
How swift the abasement follows! But few years,
And we stood eminent. Great men were ours,
Of virtue stern, and armed with mightiest powers!
How have we sunk below our proper spheres!
No Heroes, Virtues, Men! But in their place,
The nimble marmozet and magpie men;
Creatures that only mock and mimic, when
They run astride the shoulders of the race;
Democracy, in vanity elate,
Clothing but sycophants in robes of state.

♦

Sonnet—The Ship of State

Here lie the peril and necessity
That need a race of giants—a great realm,
With not one noble leader at the helm;
And the great Ship of State still driving high,
'Midst breakers, on a lee shore—to the rocks.
With ever and anon most terrible shocks—
The crew aghast, and fear in every eye.
Yet is the gracious Providence still nigh;
And, if our cause be just, our hearts be true,
We shall save goodly ship and gallant crew,
Nor suffer shipwreck of our liberty!
It needs that as a people we arise,
With solemn purpose that even fate defies,
And brave all perils with unblenching eye!

♦

The Avatar of Hell

Six thousand years of commune, God with man,—
Two thousand years of Christ; yet from such roots,
Immortal, earth reaps only bitterest fruits!
The fiends rage now as when they first began!
Hate, Lust, Greed, Vanity, triumphant still,
Yell, shout, exult, and lord o'er human will!
The sun moves back! The fond convictions felt,
That, in the progress of the race, we stood,
Two thousand years of height above the flood
Before the day's experience sink and melt,
As frost beneath the fire! and what remains
Of all our grand ideals and great gains,
With Goth, Hun, Vandal, warring in their pride,
While the meek Christ is hourly crucified!

♦

Battle Hymn

LORD of Hosts, that beholds us in battle, defending
The homes of our sires 'gainst the hosts of the foe,
Send us help on the wings of thy angels descending,
And shield from his terrors, and baffle his blow.
Warm the faith of our sons, till they flame as the iron,
Red-glowing from the fire-forge, kindled by zeal;
Make them forward to grapple the hordes that environ,
In the storm-rush of battle, through forests of steel!

Teach them, Lord, that the cause of their country makes
    glorious
The martyr who falls in the front of the fight;—
That the faith which is steadfast makes ever victorious
The arm which strikes boldly defending the right;—
That the zeal, which is roused by the wrongs of a nation,
Is a war-horse that sweeps o'er the field as his own;
And the Faith, which is winged by the soul's approbation,
Is a warrior, in proof, that can ne'er be o'erthrown.

♦

The Mountain Partisan

My rifle, pouch, and knife!
My steed! And then we part!
One loving kiss, dear wife,
One press of heart to heart!
Cling to me yet awhile,
But stay the sob, the tear!
Smile—only try to smile—
And I go without a fear.

Our little cradled boy,
He sleeps—and in his sleep,
Smiles, with an angel joy,
Which tells thee not to weep.
I'll kneel beside, and kiss—
He will not wake the while,
Thus dreaming of the bliss,
That bids thee, too, to smile.

Think not, dear wife, I go,
With a light thought at my heart:
'Tis a pang akin to woe,
That fills me as we part;
But when the wolf was heard
To howl around our lot,
Thou know'st, dear mother—bird,

I slew him on the spot!
Aye, panther, wolf, and bear,
Have perish'd 'neath my knife;
Why tremble, then, with fear,
When now I go, my wife?
Shall I not keep the peace,
That made our cottage dear;
And 'till these wolf—curs cease
Shall I be housing here?

One loving kiss, dear wife,
One press of heart to heart;
Then for the deadliest strife,
For freedom I depart!
I were of little worth,
Were these Yankee wolves left free
To ravage 'round our hearth,
And bring one grief to thee!

God's blessing on thee, wife,
Blessing on the young;
Pray for me through the strife,
And teach our infant's tongue.
Whatever haps in fight,
I shall be true to thee—
To the home of our delight—
To my people of the free.

♦

Ode—Our City By The Sea

(1863)

Our City by the Sea,
   As the Rebel City known,
With a soul and spirit free
   As the waves that make her zone,
     Stands in wait
     For the Fate
   From the angry arm of Hate;
But she nothing fears the terror of his blow;
   She hath garrisoned her walls,
   And for every son that falls,
   She will spread a thousand palls
     For the foe!

To the brave old City, joy!
   For that the felon race,
Commissioned to destroy,
   Hath fled in sore disgrace!
     That our sons
     At their guns,
   Have beat back the modem Huns—
Have maintained their household fanes and their fires;
   And, free from taint and scaith,
   Have kept the fame and faith
   (And will keep, through blood and death)
     Of their sires!

To the Lord of Hosts, the Glory,
    For His the arm and might,
That have writ for us the story,
    And have borne us through the fight!
        His our shield,
        In that field;
    Voice, that bade us never yield:
Oh! had He not been with us through the terrors of that day?
    His strength hath made us strong,
    Cheer'd the Right and crushed the Wrong,
    To His Temple let us throng—
        PRAISE AND PRAY!

♦

Fort Wagner

Glory unto the gallant boys who stood
At Wagner, and, unflinching, sought the van;
Dealing fierce blows, and shedding precious blood,
For homes as precious, and dear rights of man!
They've won the meed, and they shall have the glory;—
Song, with melodious memories, shall repeat
The legend, which shall grow to themes for story,
Told through long ages, and forever sweet!

High honour to our youth—our sons and brothers,
Georgians and Carolinians, where they stand!
They will not shame their birthrights, or their mothers,
But keep, through storm, the bulwarks of the land!
They feel that they must conquer! Not to do it,
Were worse than death—perdition! Should they fail,
The innocent races yet unborn shall rue it,
The whole world feel the wound, and nations wail!

No! They must conquer in the breach or perish!
Assured, in the last consciousness of breath,
That love shall deck their graves, and memory cherish
Their deeds, with honours that shall sweeten death!
They shall have trophies in long future hours,
And loving recollections, which shall be
Green as the summer leaves, and fresh as flowers,
That, through all seasons, bloom eternally!

Their memories shall be monuments, to rise
Next those of mightiest martyrs of the past;
Beacons, when angry tempests sweep the skies,
And feeble souls bend crouching to the blast!
A shrine for thee, young Cheves, well devoted,
Most worthy of a great, illustrious sire;—
A niche for thee, young Haskell, nobly noted,
When skies and seas around thee shook with fire!

And others as well chronicled shall be!
What though they fell with unrecorded name—
They live among the archives of the free,
With proudest title to undying fame!
The unchisell'd marble under which they sleep,
Shall tell of heroes, fearless still of fate;
Not asking if their memories shall keep,
But if they nobly served, and saved, the State!

For thee, young Fortress Wagner—
Thou shalt wear Green laurels, worthy of the names that now,
Thy sister forts of Moultrie, Sumter, bear!
See that thou lift'st, for aye, as proud a brow!
And thou shalt be, to future generations,
A trophied monument; whither men shall come
In homage; and report to distant nations,
A shrine, which foes shall never make a TOMB!

♦

Not Doubtful of Your Fatherland

Not doubtful of your fatherland,
Or of the God who gave it;
On, Southrons! 'gainst the hireling band
That struggle to enslave it;
Ring boldly out Your battle—shout,
Charge fiercely 'gainst these felon hordes:
One hour of strife
Is freedom's life,
And glory hangs upon your swords!

A thousand mothers' matron eyes,
Wives, sisters, daughters weeping,
Watch, where your virgin banner flies,
To battle fiercely sweeping:
Though science fails,
The steel prevails,
When hands that wield, own hearts of oak:
These, though the wall
Of stone may fall,
Grow stronger with each hostile stroke.

The faith that feels its cause as true,
The virtue to maintain it;
The soul to brave, the will to do,—
These seek the fight, and gain it!
The precious prize

Before your eyes,
The all that life conceives of charm,
Home, freedom, life,
Child, sister, wife,
All rest upon your soul and arm!

And what the foe, the felon race,
That seek your subjugation?
The scum of Europe, her disgrace,
The lepers of the nation.
And what the spoil
That tempts their toil,
The bait that goads them on to fight?
Lust, crime, and blood,
Each fiendish mood
That prompts and follows appetite.

Shall such prevail, and shall you fail,
Asserting cause so holy?
With souls of might, go, seek the fight,
And crush these wretches lowly.
On, with the cry,
To do or die,
As did, in darker days, your sires,
Nor stay the blow,
Till every foe,
Down stricken, in your path, expires!

♦

Sacrifice

Another victim for the sacrifice!
Oh! my own mother South,
How terrible this wail above thy youth,
Dying at the cannon's mouth,—
And for no crime—no vice—
No scheme of selfish greed—no avarice,
Or insolent ambition, seeking power;—
But that, with resolute soul and will sublime,
They made their proud election to be free,—
To leave a grand inheritance to time,
And to their sons and race, of liberty!
Oh! widow'd woman, sitting in thy weeds,
With thy young brood around thee, sad and lone—
Thy fancy sees thy hero where he bleeds,
And still thou hear'st his moan!
Dying he calls on thee—again—again!
With blessing and fond memories. Be of cheer;
He has not died—he did not bless—in vain:
For, in the eternal rounds of God, He squares
The account with sorrowing hearts; and soothes the fears,
And leads the orphans home, and dries the widow's tears.

♦

South Carolina

MY brave old Country! I have watched thee long
Still ever first to rise against the wrong;
To check the usurper in his giant stride,
And brave his terrors and abase his pride;
Foresee the insidious danger ere it rise,
And warn the heedless and inform the wise;
Scorning the lure, the bribe, the selfish game,
Which, through the office, still becomes the shame;
Thou stood'st aloof—superior to the fate
That would have wrecked thy freedom as a State.
In vain the despot's threat, his cunning lure;
Too proud thy spirit, and thy heart too pure;
Thou hadst no quest but freedom, and to be
In conscience well—assured, and people free.
The statesman's lore was thine, the patriot's aim,
These kept thee virtuous, and preserved thy fame;
The wisdom still for council, the brave voice,
That thrills a people till they all rejoice.
These were thy birthrights; and two centuries pass'd,
As, at the first, still find thee at the last;
Supreme in council, resolute in will,
Pure in thy purpose—independent still!

The great good counsels, the examples brave,
Won from the past, not buried in its grave,
Still warm your soul with courage—still impart

Wisdom to virtue, valor to the heart!
Still first to check th' encroachment—to declare
"Thus far I no further, shall the assailant dare;"
Thou keep'st thy ermine white, thy State secure,
Thy fortunes prosperous, and thy freedom sure ;
No glozing art deceives thee to thy bane;
The tempter and the usurper strive in vain!
Thy spear's first touch unfolds the fiendish form,
And first, with fearless breast, thou meet'st the storm;
Though hosts assail thee, thou thyself a host,
Prepar'st to meet the invader on the coast:
Thy generous sons contending which shall be
First in the phalanx, gathering by the sea;
No dastard fear appals them, as they teach
How best to hurl the bolt, or man the breach!

Great Soul in little frame—the hope of man
Exults, when such as thou art in the van!
Unshaken, unbeguiled, unslaved, unbought,
Thy fame shall brighten with each battle fought;
True to the examples of the past, thou'lt be,
For the long future, best security.

♦ ♦ ♦

CARRIE BELLE SINCLAIR (1839—1883) of Georgia served as a nurse in the Confederate hospitals in Savannah. She was a niece of the inventor Robert Fulton. Much of her verse was set to familiar Confederate music.

The Homespun Dress

Oh, yes, I am a Southern girl,

And glory in the name,

And boast it with far greater pride

Than glittering wealth and fame.

We envy not the Northern girl,

Her robes of beauty rare,

Though diamonds grace her snowy neck,

And pearls bedeck her hair.

CHORUS—

Hurrah! Hurrah!

For the sunny South so dear;

Three cheers for the homespun dress

The Southern ladies wear!

The homespun dress is plain, I know,

My hat's palmetto, too;

But then it shows what Southern girls

For Southern rights will do.

We send the bravest of our land,

To battle with the foe

And we will lend a helping hand—
We love the South, you know.

CHORUS—
Hurrah! Hurrah!
For the sunny South so dear;
Three cheers for the homespun dress
The Southern ladies wear!

Now Northern goods are out of date;
And since old Abe's blockade,
We Southern girls can be content
With goods that's Southern made.
We send our sweethearts to the war;
But, dear girls, never mind—
Your soldier—love will ne'er forget
The girl he left behind.

CHORUS—
Hurrah! Hurrah!
For the sunny South so dear;
Three cheers for the homespun dress
The Southern ladies wear!

The soldier is the lad for me—
A brave heart I adore;

And when the sunny South is free,
And when fighting is no more,
I'll choose me then a lover brave
From all that gallant band;
The soldier lad I love the best
Shall have my heart and hand.

CHORUS—
Hurrah! Hurrah!
For the sunny South so dear;
Three cheers for the homespun dress
The Southern ladies wear!

The Southern land's a glorious land,
And has a glorious cause;
Then cheer, three cheers for Southern rights,
And for the Southern boys!
We scorn to wear a bit of silk,
A bit of Northern lace,
But make our homespun dresses up,
And wear them with a grace.

CHORUS—
Hurrah! Hurrah!
For the sunny South so dear;
Three cheers for the homespun dress
The Southern ladies wear!

And now, young man, a word to you:
If you would win the fair,
Go to the field where Honour calls,
And win your lady there.
Remember that our brightest smiles
Are for the true and brave,
And that our tears are all for those
Who fill a soldier's grave.

CHORUS—
Hurrah! Hurrah!
For the sunny South so dear;
Three cheers for the homespun dress
The Southern ladies wear!

♦

Georgia, My Georgia!

Hark! 'tis the cannon's deafening roar,
That sounds along thy sunny shore,
And thou shalt lie in chains no more,
My wounded, bleeding Georgia!
Then arm each youth and patriot sire,
Light up the patriotic fire,
And bid the zeal of those ne'er tire,
Who strike for thee, my Georgia!

On thee is laid oppression's hand,
Around thy altars foemen stand,
To scatter freedom's gallant band,
And lay thee low, my Georgia!
But thou hast noble sons, and brave,
The Stars and Bars above thee wave,
And here we'll make oppression's grave,
Upon the soil of Georgia!

We bow at Liberty's fair shrine,
And kneel in holy love at thine,
And while above our stars still shine,
We'll strike for them and Georgia!
Thy woods with victory shall resound,
Thy brow shall be with laurels crowned,
And peace shall spread her wings around
My own, my sunny Georgia!

Yes, these shall teach thy foes to feel
That Southern hearts, and Southern steel,
Will make them in submission kneel
Before the sons of Georgia!
And thou shalt see thy daughters, too,
With pride and patriotism true,
Arise with strength to dare and do,
Ere they shall conquer Georgia:

Thy name shall be a name of pride—
Thy heroes all have nobly died,
That thou mayst be the spotless bride
Of Liberty, my Georgia!
Then wave thy sword and banner high,
And louder raise the battle—cry,
'Till shouts of victory reach the sky,
And thou art free, my Georgia!

♦ ♦ ♦

HENRY THROOP STANTON (1834—1899) of Kentucky was a lawyer, newspaper editor, and Confederate officer. After the war he published verse, mostly of everyday life, in two volumes. Stanton was the poet speaker at the dedication of a Confederate monument in Chicago in 1895. He became quite a popular poet in the later 19th century as "The Moneyless Man."

The Bivouac

A soldier lay on the frozen ground,
With only a blanket tightened around
His weary and wasted frame;
Down at his feet, the fitful light
Of fading coals in the freezing night
Fell as a mockery on the sight,
A heatless, purple flame.

All day long, with his heavy load,
Weary and sore, in the mountain road,
And over the desolate plain;
All day long, through the crusted mud,
Over the snow, and through the flood,
Marking his way with a track of blood
He followed the winding train.

Nothing to eat at the bivouac
But a frozen crust in his haversack—
The half of a comrade's store
A crust, that, after a longer fast,
Some pampered spaniel might have passed,

Knowing that morsel to be the last
That lay at his master's door.

No other sound on his slumber fell
Than the lonesome tread of the sentinel—
That equal, measured pace—
And the wind that came from the cracking pine,
And the dying oak, and the swinging vine,
In many a weary, weary line,
To his pale and hollow face.

But the soldier slept, and his dreams were bright
As the rosy glow of his bridal—night,
With the angel on his breast;
For he passed away from the wintry gloom
To the softened light of a distant room,
Where a cat sat purring upon the loom,
And his weary heart was blest.

His children came, two blue—eyed girls,
With laughing lips and sunny curls,
And cheeks of ruddy glow;
And the mother pale, but lovely now,
As when, upon her virgin brow
He proudly sealed his early vow,
In summer, long ago.

But the reveille wild, in the morning gray,
Startled the beautiful vision away,
As a frightened bird in the night;
And it seemed to the soldier's misty brain
But the shrill tattoo that sounded again,
And he turned with a dull, uneasy pain,
To the camp—fire's dying light.

♦

The Little Boy Guiding the Plow

When a bugle—note rang in the quivering trees,
And a drum beat the nation to arms,
Our people came up from the shore of the seas,
And away from their blue—mountain farms;
All stalwart and strong as the hardy old pines,
Or the wave—breaking rocks of the shore,
They came in their long gleaming columns and lines,
Till the bugle—note sounded no more.
There are hearts in the ranks, as light as the foam;
There are those of a gloomier brow;
And some who have left but a mother at home,
With her little boy guiding the plow.

There are silver—haired men, the tide in their veins
Leaping down the red alleys of youth,
All fresh as the water—fall thrown to the plains,
And as pure as the beautiful truth;
There are sons, too, and sires—the old and the young—
In the midnight and morning of life,
Who came from the hills and the valleys among,
To be first in the glorious strife;
And many, how many beneath the blue dome,
Are bending in solitude now,
To plead for the weal of a mother at home,
And her little boy guiding the plow!

Oh, the pang of his heart, and the keenest of all
That a wandering father may know,
Is the vision of home with its agony—call,
Its hunger and shivering woe;
And who would not chafe in the sacredest chain
At a memory bitter as this,
Though he knew in his heart that each moment of pain
Would but hallow his future to bliss?
And who would not weep in a vision of gloom.
When the Evil One whispered him how
The toil grew apace to the mother at home,
And her little boy guiding the plow?

But courage, keep courage, oh, parent away!
Be noble, and faithful, and brave!
And the midnight shall pass, and the glorious day
Shall be shed over tyranny's grave!
Though a desolate thing is a fenceless farm,
And as dreary, a furrowless field,
Still, God in his mercy shall strengthen the arm
Of the little boy asking a yield;
And the stubbornest clay shall be as the loam,
When the patriot spirit shall bow,
And ask for a friend to the mother at home,
And her little boy guiding the plow.

Oh, God will be kind to the needy and poor
Who shall suffer from tyranny's hand;
His foot-print shall be by the loneliest door,
And his bounty shall cover the land;
And broken the glebe in the valley and mead,
Where the poorest and weakest shall be,
And plenty shall spring of the promising seed,
Till a people shall live to be free;
And never, oh, never shall tyranny come,
With iron—bound bosom and brow—
May God give him back to the mother at home,
And her little boy guiding the plow.

◆ ◆ ◆

OLIVIA TULLY THOMAS of Mississippi. Not much has been found about this poet.

The Southern Republic

In the galaxy of nations,
A nation's flag's unfurled,
Transcending in its martial pride
The nations of the world.
Though born of war, baptized in blood,
Yet mighty from the time,
Like fabled phoenix, forth she stood—
Dismembered, yet sublime.

And braver heart, and bolder hand,
Ne'er formed a fabric fair
As Southern wisdom can command,
And Southern valour rear.
Though kingdoms scorn to own her sway,
Or recognise her birth,
The land blood—bought for Liberty
Will reign supreme on earth.

Clime of the Sun! Home of the Brave!
Thy sons are bold and free,
And pour life's crimson tide to save
Their birthright, Liberty!

Their fertile fields and sunny plains
That yield the wealth alone,
That's coveted for greedy gains
By despots—and a throne!

Proud country! battling, bleeding, torn,
Thy altars desolate;
Thy lovely dark—eyed daughters mourn
At war's relentless fate;
And widow's prayers, and orphan's tears,
Her homes will consecrate,
While more than brass or marble rears
The trophy of her great.

Oh! land that boasts each gallant name
And hosts of valiant sons whose fame
Extends beyond the sea;
Far rather let thy plains become,
From gulf to mountain cave,
One honoured sepulchre and tomb,
Than we the tyrant's slave!

Fair, favoured land! thou mayst be free,
Redeemed by blood and war;
Through agony and gloom we see
Thy hope—a glimmering star;

Thy banner, too, may proudly float,
A herald on the seas—
Thy deeds of daring worlds remote
Will emulate and praise!

But who can paint the impulse pure,
That thrills and nerves thy brave
To deeds of valour, that secure
The rights their fathers gave?
Crowned with the warrior's wreath,
From beds of fame their proud refrain
Was "Liberty or Death!"

♦

When Peace Returns

When "war has smoothed his wrinkled front,"
And meek—eyed peace returning,
Has brightened hearts that long were wont
To sigh in grief and mourning—
How blissful then will be the day
When, from the wars returning,
The weary soldier wends his way
To dear ones that are yearning.

To clasp in true love's fond embrace,
To gaze with looks so tender
Upon the war—worn form and face
Of Liberty's defender;
To count with pride each cruel scar,
That mars the manly beauty,
Of him who proved so brave in war,
So beautiful in duty.

When peace returns, throughout our land,
Glad shouts of welcome render
The gallant few of Freedom's band
Whose cry was "no surrender;"
Who battled bravely to be free
From tyranny's oppressions,
And won, for Southern chivalry,
The homage of all nations!

And when, again, in Southern bowers
The ray of peace is shining,
Her maidens gather fairest flowers,
And honour 's wreaths are twining, To bind the brows
    victorious
On many a field so gory,
Whose names, renowned and glorious,
Shall live in song and story.
Then will affection's tear be shed,
And pity, joy restraining,
For those, the lost, lamented dead,
Are all beyond our plaining;
They fell in manhood's prime and might;
And we should not weep the story
That tells of Fame, a sacred light,
Above each grave of glory!

(From Granada, Miss., *Picket*.)

♦ ♦ ♦

JOHN REUBEN THOMPSON (1823—1873) of Virginia was the founder and editor of Southern literary magazines and a friend and sponsor of Edgar Allan Poe. Thompson spent the war in England writing articles in support of the Confederacy, becoming friends with Thomas Carlyle and Alfred Lord Tennyson. In his postwar years he was editor of the *New York Post*, an indication of how much Confederate sympathy there was there. Captain William Latane' was the only Confederate killed in Jeb Stuart's famous ride around McClellan's army. His brother took him to be buried and became a prisoner of war. No clergymen were allowed through the Yankee lines to conduct a burial service so Latane' was laid to rest by two ladies who read the service. William D. Washington's painting "The Burial of Latane'" became famous from engravings spread throughout the South. Thompson's "On to Richmond" and "A Farewell to Pope" are humourous account of Yankee bragging followed by defeat at First and Second Manassas.

The Burial of Latane'

The combat ranged not long, but our's the day;

    And through the hosts that compassed us around

Our little band rode proudly on its way,

    Leaving one gallant comrade, glory-crowned,

Unburied on the field he died to gain,

Single of all his men amid the hostile slain.

One moment on the battle's edge he stood,

    Hope's halo like a helmet round his hair,

The next beheld him, dabbled in his blood,

    Prostrate in death, and yet in death how fair!

Even thus he passed through the red gate of strife,

From earthly crowns and palms to an immortal life.

A brother bore his body from the field
    And gave it unto stranger's hands that closed
The calm, blue eyes on earth forever sealed,
    And tenderly the slender limbs composed:
Strangers, yet sisters, who with Mary's love,
Sat by the open tomb and weeping looked above.

A little child strewed roses on his bier,
    Pale roses, not more stainless than his soul.
Nor yet more fragrant than his life sincere
    That blossomed with good actions, brief, but whole:
The aged matron and the faithful slave
Approached with reverent feet the hero's lowly grave.

No man of God might say the burial rite
    Above the "rebel"—thus declared the foe
That blanched before him in the deadly fight.
    But woman's voice, in accents soft and low,
Trembling with pity, touched with pathos, read
Over his hallowed dust the ritual for the dead.

"Tis sown in weakness, it is raised in power,"
    Softly the promise floated on the air,
And the sweet breathings of the sunset hour
    Came back responsive to the mourner's prayer;
Gently they laid him underneath the sod,
And left him with his fame, his country, and his God.

Let us not weep for him whose deeds endure,
　　So young, so brave, so beautiful, he died;
As he had wished to die; the past is sure,
　　Whatever yet or so now may betide
Those who still linger by the stormy shore,
Change cannot harm him now nor fortune touch him more.

And when Virginia, leaning on her spear,
　　Victrix et vidua; the conflict done,
Shall raise her mailed hand to wipe the tear
　　That starts as she recalls each martyred son,
No prouder memory her breast shall sway,
Than thine, our early—lost, lamented Latane'.

♦

Coercion: A Poem for Then and Now

Who talks of coercion? who dares to deny
A resolute people the right to be free?
Let him blot out forever one star from the sky,
Or curb with his fetter the wave of the sea!

Who prates of coercion? Can love be restored
To bosoms where only resentment may dwell?
Can peace upon earth be proclaimed by the sword,
Or good—will among men be established by shell?

Shame! Shame!—that the statesman and trickster, forsooth,
Should have for a crisis no other recourse,
Beneath the fair day-spring of light and of truth,
Than the old *brutum fulmen* of tyranny—force!

From the holes where fraud, falsehood, and hate slink away—
From the crypt in which error lies buried in chains—
This foul apparition stalks forth to the day,
And would ravage the land which his presence profanes.

Could you conquer us, men of the North—could you bring
Desolation and death on our homes as a flood—
Can you hope the pure lily, affection, will spring
From ashes all reeking and sodden with blood?

Could you brand us as villains and serfs, know ye not
What fierce, sullen hatred lurks under the scar?
How loyal to Hapsburg is Venice, I wot!
How dearly the Pole loves his father, the Czar!

But 'twere well to remember this land of the sun
Is a *nutrix leonum*, and suckles a race
Strong-armed, lion-hearted, and banded as one,
Who brook not oppression and know not disgrace.

And well may the schemers in office beware
The swift retribution that waits upon crime,
When the lion, RESISTANCE, shall leap from his lair,
With a fury that renders his vengeance sublime.

Once, men of the North, we were brothers, and still,
Though brothers no more, we would gladly be friends;
Nor join in a conflict accursed, that must fill
With ruin the country on which it descends.

But, if smitten with blindness, and mad with the rage
The gods gave to all whom they wished to destroy,
You would act a new Iliad, to darken the age
With horrors beyond what is told us of Troy—

If, deaf as the adder itself to the cries,
When wisdom, humanity, justice implore,
You would have our proud eagle to feed on the eyes
Of those who have taught him so grandly to soar—

If there be to your malice no limit imposed,
And you purpose hereafter to rule with the rod
The men upon whom you already have closed
Our goodly domain and the temples of God:

To the breeze then your banner dishonoured unfold,
And, at once, let the tocsin be sounded afar;
We greet you, as greeted the Swiss, Charles the Bold—
With a farewell to peace and a welcome to war!

For the courage that clings to our soil, ever bright,
Shall catch inspiration from turf and from tide;
Our sons unappalled shall go forth to the fight,
With the smile of the fair, the pure kiss of the bride;

And the bugle its echoes shall send through the past,
In the trenches of Yorktown to waken the slain;
While the sod of King's Mountain shall heave at the blast,
And give up its heroes to glory again.

◆

On to Richmond

MAJOR—GENERAL SCOTT
An order had got
To push on the columns to Richmond;
For loudly went forth,
From all parts of the North,
The cry that an end of the war must be made
In time for the regular yearly Fall Trade;
Mr. Greeley spoke freely about the delay,
The Yankees "to hum" were all hot for the fray:
The chivalrous Grow
Declared they were slow,
And therefore the order
To march from the border
And make an excursion to Richmond.

Major—General Scott
Most likely was not
Very loth to obey this instruction, I wot;
In his private opinion
The Ancient Dominion
Deserved to be pillaged, her sons to be shot,
And the reason is easily noted;
Though this part of the earth
Had given him birth,
And medals and swords,
Inscribed in fine words,

It never for Winfield had voted.

Besides, you must know, that our First Commanders

Had sworn quite as hard as the Army in Flanders,

With his finest of armies and proudest of navies,

To wreak his old grudge against Jefferson Davis.

Then, "forward the column," he said to McDowell;

And the Zouaves with a shout,

Most fiercely cried out,

"To Richmond or h—ll" (I omit here the vowel),

And Winfield he ordered his carriage and four,

A dashing turnout, to be brought to the door,

For a pleasant excursion to Richmond.

Major—General Scott

Had there on the spot

A splendid array

To plunder and slay;

In the camp he might boast

Such a numerous host,

As he never had yet

In the battle-field set;

Every class and condition of Northern society,

Were in for the trip, a most varied variety;

In the camp he might hear every lingo in vogue;

"The sweet German accent, the rich Irish brogue."

The beautiful boy

From the banks of the Shannon,

Was there to employ
His excellent cannon,
And besides the long files of dragoons and artillery,
The Zouaves and Hussars,
All the children of Mars,
There were barbers and cooks
And writers of books,—
The chef de cuisine with his French bills of fare,
And the artists to dress the young officers' hair.
And the scribblers were ready at once to prepare
An eloquent story
Of conquest and glory;
And servants with numberless baskets of Sillery,
Though Wilson, the Senator, followed the train,
At a distance quite safe, to "conduct the champagne;"
While the fields were so green, and the sky was so blue,
There was certainly nothing more pleasant to do
On this pleasant excursion to Richmond.

In Congress the talk, as I said, was of action,
To crush out instanter the traitorous faction.
In the press, and the mess,
They would hear of nothing less
Than to make the advance, spite of rhyme or of reason,
And at once put an end to this insolent treason.
There was Greeley,
And Ely,

The bloodthirsty Grow,
And Hickman (the rowdy, not Hickman the beau,)
And that terrible Baker
Who would seize on the South, every acre,
And Webb, who would drive us all into the Gulf, or
Some nameless locality smelling of sulphur;
And with all this bold crew
Nothing would do,
While the fields were so green, and the sky was so blue,
But to march on directly to Richmond.

Then the gallant McDowell,
Drove madly the rowel
Of spur that had never been "won" by him,
In the flank of his steed,
To accomplish a deed,
Such as never before had been done by him;
And the battery called Sherman's
Was wheeled into line,
While the beer—drinking Germans
From Neckar and Rhine,
With minie and yager,
Came on with a swagger,
Full of fury and lager,
(The day and the pageant were equally fine.)
Oh! the fields were so green, and the sky was so blue,
Indeed 'twas a spectacle pleasant to view,
As the column pushed onward to Richmond.

Ere the march was begun.
In a spirit of fun,
General Scott in a speech
Said the army should teach
The Southrons the lesson of laws to obey,
And just before dusk of the third or fourth day,
Should joyfully march into Richmond.

He spoke of their drill,
And their courage and skill,
And declared that the ladies of Richmond would rave
O'er such matchless perfection, and gracefully wave
In rapture their delicate kerchiefs in air
At their morning parades on the Capitol Square.
But alack! and alas!
Mark what soon came to pass,
When this army, in spite of his flatteries,
Amid war's loudest thunder
Must stupidly blunder
Upon those accursed "masked batteries."
Then Beauregard came,
Like a tempest of flame,
To consume them in wrath
In their perilous path;
And Johnston bore down, in a whirlwind to sweep
Their ranks from the field
Where their doom had been sealed,
As the storm rushes over the face of the deep!

While swift on the centre our President passed,
And the foe might descry,
In the glance of his eye,
The light that once blazed on Diomed's crest.
McDowell! McDowell! weep, weep for the day
When the Southrons you meet in their battle array;
To your confident hosts with its bullet and steel
'Twas worse than Culloden to luckless Lochiel.
Oh! the generals were green and old Scott is now blue,
And a terrible business, McDowell, to you,
Was that pleasant excursion to Richmond.

♦

A Farewell to Pope

"Hats off' in the crowd, "Present arms" in the line!
Let the standards all bow, and the sabres incline—
Roll, drums, the Rogue's March, while the conqueror goes,
Whose eyes have seen only "the backs of his foes"—
Through a thicket of laurel, a whirlwind of cheers,
His vanishing form from our gaze disappears;
Henceforth with the savage Dacotahs to cope,
Abiit, evasit, erupit—John Pope.

He came out of the West, like the young Lochinvar,
Compeller of fate and controller of war,
Videre et vincere, simply to see,
And straightway to conquer Hill, Jackson and Lee,
And old Abe at the White House, like Kilmansegg *père*,
With a monkeyish grin and beatified air,
"Seemed washing his hands with invisible soap,"
As with eager attention he listened to Pope.

He came—and the poultry was swept by his sword,
Spoons, liquors, and furniture went by the board;
He saw—at a distance, the rebels appear,
And "rode to the front," which was strangely the rear;
He conquered—truth, decency, honour full soon,
Pest, pilferer, puppy, pretender, poltroon;
And was fain from the scene of his triumphs to slope.
Sure there never was fortunate hero like Pope.

He has left us his shining example to note,
And Stuart has captured his uniform coat;
But 'tis puzzling enough, as his deeds we recall,
To tell on whose shoulders his mantle should fall;
While many may claim to deserve it, at least,
From Hunter, the Hound, down to Butler, the Beast,
None else, we can say, without risking the trope,
But himself can be parallel ever to Pope.

Like his namesake the poet of genius and fire,
He gives new expression and force to the lyre;
But in one little matter they differ, the two,
And differ, indeed, very widely, 'tis true—
While his verses gave great Alexander his fame,
'Tis our hero's reverses accomplish the same;
And fate may decree that the end of a rope
Shall award yet his highest position to Pope.

♦ ♦ ♦

MERIWETHER "JEFF" THOMPSON (1826—1876) of Missouri was before the war mayor and a leading citizen of St. Joseph, Missouri, a major depot for westward bound settlers. As a Confederate he became well known as an effective Missouri partisan, called "The Swamp Fox." He seems a natural, spontaneous and prolific poet, ready with verse for any occasion. The poems are uncollected, scattered in newspapers of the time and some in his memoirs.

Missouri, Missouri, Awake from Thy Slumber

Missouri! Missouri! Awake from thy slumber,

Hear'st thou not the hammer that rivets thy chains?

Can't the death shriek of fathers, the wail of thy mothers

The tears of thy daughters, arouse thee again?

Come! Rise in thy might, drive the Huns from thy borders,

And stand by thy Southern sons in the fight,

Pour forth all thy men, to help them to battle

For Freedom, for Glory, for Justice, for Right.

Let thy watchfires glow, and thy bugles blast high

O'er thy mountains and valleys, o'er the prairies and lea,

Then the glad shout shall ring o'er the prairies and streams,

Hail! Brothers Hail! Missouri is Free!

◆

A Rebel

My father's father was a rebel,
And Mother's father was a rebel too,
So when the South called out her soldiers
Pray what else would you have me do?
But buckle on my father's sabre,
And seize at once his trusty gun,
And strike a blow for Southern freedom,
Like old Virginia's faithful son?

♦

Damn It, Let It Rip

Come comrades open wide your eyes, and listen while I sing;

I'll promise that you'll shed no tears, about the news I bring,

For all seems bright and hopeful too, in our fair Southern land,

And all that we now have to do is keep our gizzards full of sand.

For we of all the noble hosts, that strikes for Southern Rights

Need patience more, and suffer most being kept away from fights

Where Glory Honour and our hate would sweeten every blow,

While all we do is DAMN THE FATE that will not let us go.

♦

Home, Sweet Home

My dear wife waits my coming,
My children lisp my name,
Kind friends would bid me welcome to my dear home again,
My father's grave is on the hill, my boys lie in the vale,
I love each rock and murmuring rill,
Each mountain, wood and dale.
I'll suffer hardships, toil and pain,
For a good time's sure to come,
I'll battle long that I may gain my freedom and my home
I will return though foes may stand, disputing every rod;
My own dear home, my native land,
I'll win you—by God!

♦ ♦ ♦

FRANCIS ORRAY TICKNOR (1822—1876) of Georgia was a highly regarded physician trained in Philadelphia and a contributor of scientific articles to agricultural publications. He also wrote some of the most memorable Confederate poetry. His "Little Giffen" is certainly one of the finest poems of the War.

The Old Rifleman

Now bring me out my buckskin suit!

My pouch and powder, too!

We'll see if seventy-six can shoot

As sixteen used to do.

Old Bess! we've kept our barrels bright!

Our trigger quick and true!

As far, if not as fine a sight,

As long ago we drew!

And pick me out a trusty flint!

A real white and blue,

Perhaps 'twill win the other tint

Before the hunt is through!

Give boys your brass percussion caps!

Old "shut-pan" suits as well!

There's something in the sparks: perhaps

There's something in the smell!

We've seen the red-coat Briton bleed!
The red-skin Indian, too!
We've never thought to draw a bead
On Yankee-doodle-doo!

But, Bessie I bless your dear old heart!
Those days are mostly done;
And now we must revive the art
Of shooting on the run!

If Doodle must be meddling, why,
There's only this to do—
Select the black spot in his eye,
And let the daylight through!

And if he doesn't like the way
That Bess presents the view,
He'll maybe change his mind, and stay
Where the good Doodles do!

We'll teach these shot-gun boys the tricks
By which a war is won;
Especially how Seventy-six
Took Tories on the run.

◆

Little Giffen

Out of the focal and foremost fire,
Out of the hospital walls as dire,
Smitten of grapeshot and gangrene,
(Eighteenth battle and he sixteen) —
Specter! such as you seldom see,
Little Giffen of Tennessee.

'Take him and welcome,' the surgeon said;
Little the doctor can help the dead!
So we took him, and brought him where
The balm was sweet in the summer air;
And we laid him down on a wholesome bed —
Utter Lazarus, heel to head!

And we watched the war with abated breath,
Skeleton boy against skeleton death!
Months of torture, how many such?
Weary weeks of the stick and crutch;
And still a glint in the steel—blue eye
Told of a spirit that wouldn't die.

And didn't. Nay! more! in death's despite
The crippled skeleton learned to write —
'Dear Mother!' at first, of course, and then
'Dear Captain!' inquiring about the men.

Captain's answer: Of eighty and five,
Giffen and I are left alive.

Word of gloom from the war, one day;
Johnston pressed at the front, they say; —
Little Giffen was up and away!
A tear, his first, as he bade good-by,
Dimmed the glint of his steel—blue eye.
'I'll write, if spared!' There was news of fight,
But none of Giffen — he did not write!

I sometimes fancy that were I King
Of the Princely Knights of the Golden Ring,
With the song of the minstrel in mine ear,
And the tender legend that trembles here,
I'd give the best on his bended knee —
The whitest soul of my chivalry —
For 'Little Giffen' of Tennessee.

◆

Our Left

From dawn to dark they stood
That long midsummer day,
While fierce and fast
The battle blast
Swept rank on rank away.

From dawn to dark they fought,
With legions torn and cleft;
And still the wide
Black battle—tide
Poured deadlier on "Our Left."

They closed each ghastly gap;
They dressed each shattered rank;
They knew—how well—
That Freedom fell
With that exhausted flank.

"Oh, for a thousand men
Like these that melt away!"
And down they came,
With steel and flame,
Four thousand to the fray!

Right through the blackest cloud
Their lightning path they cleft;
And triumph came
With deathless fame
To our unconquered "Left."

Ye, of your sons secure,
Ye, of your dead bereft,
Honour the brave
Who died to save
Your all upon our "Left."

♦

Loyal

To General Patrick Cleburne

The good Lord Douglas—dead of old—
In his last journeying
Wore at his heart, encased in gold,
The heart of Bruce, his king,

Through Paynim lands to Palestine—
For so his troth was plight—
To lay that gold on Christ his shrine,
Let fall what peril might.

By night and day, a weary way
Of vigil and of fight,
Where never rescue came by day,
Nor ever rest by night.

And one by one the valiant spears
Were smitten from his side,
And one by one the bitter tears
Fell for the brave that died;

Till fierce and black around his track
He saw the combat close,
And counted but the single sword
Against uncounted foes.

He drew the casket from his breast,
He bared his solemn brow!
Oh, foremost of the kingliest!
Go "first in battle" now!

Where leads my Lord of Bruce, the sword
Of Douglas shall not stay!
Forward! We meet at Christ His feet
In Paradise, to-day!

The casket flashed; the battle clashed,
Thundered, and rolled away;
And dead above the heart of Bruce
The heart of Douglas lay!

Loyal! Methinks the antique mould
Is lost, or theirs alone
Who sheltered Freedom's heart of gold,
Like Douglas, with their own!

♦

The Virginians of The Valley

The knightliest of the knightly race
That, since the days of old,
Have kept the lamp of chivalry
Alight in hearts of gold;
The kindliest of the kindly band
That, rarely hating ease,
Yet rode with Spotswood round the land,
And Raleigh round the seas;

Who climbed the blue Virginian hills
Against embattled foes,
And planted there, in valleys fair,
The lily and the rose;
Whose fragrance lives in many lands,
Whose beauty stars the earth,
And lights the hearths of happy homes
With loveliness and worth.

We thought they slept! —the sons who kept
The names of noble sires,
And slumbered while the darkness crept
Around their vigil-fires;
But, aye, the "Golden Horseshoe" knights
Their old Dominion keep,
Whose foes have found enchanted ground,
But not a knight asleep!

♦

Ora Pace

Ora Pace! Pray for Peace!
Till these times of tumult cease!
Ye with heavy hearts and eyes,
Watchers as the war—clouds rise,
Though the shadows still increase,
Gentle spirits! Pray for Peace!

Ora Pace! Ye that lift
The nation's weapons, keen and swift,
Ere ye loose the thunder, pray
That the wrath may pass away!
Ere the lightnings ye release,
Patriot statesmen, Pray for Peace!

Ora Pace! Ye that stand
The shield and summer of the land;
Though the blood is hot and high,
Bounding for the battle—cry,
Remember, boys, whose kiss ye bear,
And pray for peace, ye sons of Prayer!

Ora Pace! Who shall tread
Our Lilies, when that prayer is said?
Dark may be the sullen tide
Of the stranger's lust and pride,
But, our God shall still increase
The strength that strikes and prays for Peace.

♦ ♦ ♦

HENRY TIMROD (1828—1867) of South Carolina was known as a lyric poet before the war, but the great subject of Southern independence brought forth his best works. Timrod, though suffering from incipient tuberculosis, twice enlisted in the Confederate army but both times was discharged as unfit. Poverty and hardship endured while struggling to support his family in the ruins of Columbia hastened Timrod's death at thirty-nine. A few months before, he had written "The Ode to the Confederate Dead" for the occasion of placing flowers on the Confederate graves at Magnolia Cemetery in Charleston, until then forbidden by the U.S. Army. Some people claim to prefer the vicious and blasphemous "Battle Hymn of the Republic" or Walt Whitman's adolescent jingles, but for my money Timrod's ode (in the next volume of this series) is the most magnificent piece of literature to come out of The War.

Ethnogenesis

(1861)

I

Hath not the morning dawned with added light?

And shall not evening call another star

Out of the infinite regions of the night.

To mark this clay in Heaven? At last, we are

A nation among nations; and the world

Shall soon behold in many a distant port

Another flag unfurled!

Now, come what may, whose favor need we court?

And, under God, whose thunder need we fear?

Thank Him who placed us here

Beneath so kind a sky — the very sun
Takes part with us; and on our errands run
All breezes of the ocean; dew and rain
Do noiseless battle for us: and the Year,
And all the gentle daughters in her train,
March in our ranks, and in our service wield

    Long spears of golden grain!

A yellow blossom as her fairy shield,
June flings her azure banner to the wind,

    While in the order of their birth

Her sisters pass, and many an ample field
Grows white beneath their steps, till now, behold,

    Its endless sheets unfold

THE SNOW OF SOUTHERN SUMMERS! Let the earth
Rejoice! Beneath those fleeces soft and warm

    Our happy land shall sleep
    In a repose as deep
    As if we lay intrenched behind

Whose leagues of Russian ice and Arctic storm!

II

And what if, mad with wrongs themselves have wrought,
In their own treachery caught,
By their own fears made bold,
And leagued with him or old,

Who long since in the limits of the North
Set up his evil throne, and warred with God—
What if, both mad and blinded in their rage,
Our foes should fling us down their mortal gage,
And with a hostile step profane our sod!
We shall not shrink, my brothers, but go forth
To meet them, marshaled by the Lord of Hosts,
And overshadowed by the mighty ghosts
Of Moultrie and of Eutaw — who shall foil
Auxiliars such as these? Nor these alone,

But every stock and stone
Shall help us: but the very soil,

And all the generous wealth it gives to toil,
And all for which we love our noble land,
Shall fight beside, and through us; sea and strand.

The heart of woman, and her hand,

Tree, fruit, and flower, and every influence.

Gentle, or grave, or grand;
The winds in our defence

Shall seem to blow: to us the bills shall lend

Their firmness and their calm;

And in our stiffened sinews we shall blend

The strength of pine and palm!

III

Nor would we shun the battle-ground,
Though weak as we are strong;

Call up the clashing elements around,

And test the right and wrong!

On one side, creeds that dare to teach
What Christ and Paul refrained to preach;
Codes built upon a broken pledge,
And Charity that whets a poniard's edge;
Fair schemes that leave the neighboring poor
To starve and shiver at the schemer's door,

While in the world's most liberal ranks enrolled,
He turns some vast philanthropy to gold;
Religion, taking every moral form
But that a pure and Christian faith makes warm,
Where not to vile fanatic passion urged,
Or not in vague philosophies submerged,
Repulsive with all Pharisaic leaven,
And making laws to stay the laws of Heaven!
And on the other, scorn or sordid gain,
Unblemished honour, truth, without a stain,
Faith, justice, reverence, charitable wealth.
And, for the poor and humble, laws which give,
Not the mean right to buy the right to live,

    But life, and home, and health!

To doubt the end were want of trust in God,

    Who, if He has decreed
    That we must pass a redder sea

Than that which rang to Miriam's holy glee,

    Will surely raise at need
    A Moses with his rod!

IV

But let our fears — if fears we have — be still
And turn us to the future! Could we climb
Some mighty Alp. and view the coming time,
The rapturous sight would fill

Our Eyes with happy tears!

Not only for the glories which the years
Shall bring us: not for lands from sea to sea,
And wealth, and power, and peace,
      though these shall be;
But for the distant peoples we shall bless,
And the bushed murmurs of a world's distress;
For, to give labour to the poor,

The whole sad planet o'er,

And save from want and crime the humblest door,
Is one among the many ends for which

God makes us great and rich!

The hour perchance is not yet wholly ripe
When all shall own it, but the type
Whereby we shall be known in every land

Is that vast gulf which lips our Southern strand,
And through the cold, untempered ocean pours
Its genial streams, that far off Arctic shores
May sometimes catch upon the softened breeze
Strange tropic warmth and hint of summer seas.

♦

A Cry to Arm

Ho! woodsmen of the mountain side!
Ho! dwellers in the vales!
Ho! ye who by the chafing tide
Have roughened in the gales!
Leave barn and byre, leave kin and cot,
Lay by the bloodless spade;
Let desk, and case, and counter rot,
And burn your books of trade.

The despot roves your fairest lands;
And till he flies or fears,
Your fields must grow but armed bands,
Your sheaves be sheaves of spears!
Give up to mildew and to rust
The useless tools of gain;
And feed your country's sacred dust
With floods of crimson rain!

Come, with the weapons at your call—
With musket, pike, or knife;
He wields the deadliest blade of all
Who lightest holds his life.
The arm that drives its unbought blows
With all a patriot's scorn,
Might brain a tyrant with a rose,
Or stab him with a thorn.

Does any falter? let him turn
To some brave maiden's eyes,
And catch the holy fires that burn
In those sublunar skies.
Oh! could you like your women feel,
And in their spirit march,
A day might see your lines of steel
Beneath the victor's arch.

What hope, O God! would not grow warm
When thoughts like these give cheer?
The Lily calmly braves the storm,
And shall the Palm—tree fear?
No! rather let its branches court
The rack that sweeps the plain;
And from the Lily's regal port
Learn how to breast the strain!

Ho! woodsmen of the mountain side!
Ho! dwellers in the vales!
Ho! ye who by the roaring tide
Have roughened in the gales!
Come! flocking gayly to the fight,
From forest, hill, and lake;
We battle for our Country's right,
And for the Lily's sake!

♦

Carolina

I

The despot treads thy sacred sands,
Thy pines give shelter to his bands,
Thy sons stand by with idle hands,
    Carolina!
He breathes at ease thy airs of balm,
He scorns the lances of thy palm;
Oh! who shall break thy craven calm,
    Carolina!
Thy ancient fame is growing dim,
A spot is on thy garment's rim;
Give to the winds thy battle hymn,
    Carolina!

II

Call on thy children of the hill,
Wake swamp and river, coast and rill,
Rouse all thy strength and all thy skill,
    Carolina!
Cite wealth and science, trade and art,
Touch with thy fire the cautious mart,
And pour thee through the people's heart,
    Carolina!
Till even the coward spurns his fears,
And all thy fields and fens and meres
Shall bristle like thy palm with spears,
    Carolina!

III

Hold up the glories of thy dead;
Say how thy elder children bled,
And point to Eutaw's battle-bed,
    Carolina!
Tell how the patriot's soul was tried,
And what his dauntless breast defied;
How Rutledge ruled and Laurens died,
    Carolina!
Cry! till thy summons, heard at last,
Shall fall like Marion's bugle-blast
Re-echoed from the haunted Past,
    Carolina!

IV

I hear a murmur as of waves
That grope their way through sunless caves,
Like bodies struggling in their graves,
    Carolina!
And now it deepens; slow and grand
It swells, as, rolling to the land,
An ocean broke upon thy strand,
    Carolina!
Shout! let it reach the startled Huns!
And roar with all thy festal guns!
It is the answer of thy sons,
    Carolina!

V

They will not wait to hear thee call;
From Sachem's Head to Sumter's wall
Resounds the voice of hut and hall,
    Carolina!
No! thou hast not a stain, they say,
Or none save what the battle-day
Shall wash in seas of blood away,
    Carolina!
Thy skirts indeed the foe may part,
Thy robe be pierced with sword and dart,
They shall not touch thy noble heart,
    Carolina!

VI

Ere thou shalt own the tyrant's thrall
Ten times ten thousand men must fall;
Thy corpse may hearken to his call,
    Carolina!
When, by thy bier, in mournful throngs
The women chant thy mortal wrongs,
'Twill be their own funereal songs,
    Carolina!
From thy dead breast by ruffians trod
No helpless child shall look to God;
All shall be safe beneath thy sod,
    Carolina!

VII

Girt with such wills to do and bear,
Assured in right, and mailed in prayer,
Thou wilt not bow thee to despair,
    Carolina!
Throw thy bold banner to the breeze!
Front with thy ranks the threatening seas
Like thine own proud armorial trees,
    Carolina!
Fling down thy gauntlet to the Huns,
And roar the challenge from thy guns;
Then leave the future to thy sons,
    Carolina!

♦

The Two Armies

Two armies stand enrolled beneath
The banner with the starry wreath;
One, facing battle, blight and blast,
Through twice a hundred fields has passed;
Its deeds against a ruffian foe,
Stream, valley, hill, and mountain know,
Till every wind that sweeps the land
Goes, glory laden, from the strand.

The other, with a narrower scope,
Yet led by not less grand a hope,
Hath won, perhaps, as proud a place,
And wears its fame with meeker grace,
Wives march beneath its glittering sign,
Fond mothers swell the lovely line,
And many a sweetheart hides her blush
In the young patriot's generous flush.

No breeze of battle ever fanned
The colors of that tender band;
Its office is beside the bed,
Where throbs some sick or wounded head,
It does not court the soldier's tomb,
But plies the needle and the loom;
And, by a thousand peaceful deeds,
Supplies a struggling nation's needs.

Nor is that army's gentle might
Unfelt amid the deadly fight;
It nerves the son's, the husband's hand,
It points the lover's fearless brand;
It thrills the languid, warms the cold,
Gives even new courage to the bold;
And sometimes lifts the veriest clod
To its own lofty trust in God.

♦

Christmas

How grace this hallowed day?
Shall happy bells, from yonder ancient spire,
Send their glad greetings to each Christmas fire
Round which the children play?

Alas! for many a moon,
That tongueless tower hath cleaved the Sabbath air,
Mute as an obelisk of ice, aglare
Beneath an Arctic noon.

Shame to the foes that drown
Our psalms of worship with their impious drum,
The sweetest chimes in all the land lie dumb
In some far rustic town.

There, let us think, they keep,
Of the dead Yules which here beside the sea
They've ushered in with old-world, English glee,
Some echoes in their sleep.

How shall we grace the day?
With feast, and song, and dance, and antique sports,
And shout of happy children in the courts,
And tales of ghost and fay?

Is there indeed a door,
Where the old pastimes, with their lawful noise,
And all the merry round of Christmas joys,
Could enter as of yore?

Would not some pallid face
Look in upon the banquet, calling up
Dread shapes of battles in the wassail cup,
And trouble all the place?

How could we bear the mirth,
While some loved reveler of a year ago
Keeps his mute Christmas now beneath the snow,
In cold Virginian earth?

How shall we grace the day?
Ah! let the thought that on this holy morn
The Prince of Peace — the Prince of Peace was born,
Employ us, while we pray!

Pray for the peace which long
Hath left this tortured land, and haply now
Holds its white court on some far mountain's brow,
There hardly safe from wrong!

Let every sacred fane
Call its sad votaries to the shrine of God,
And, with the cloister and the tented sod,
Join in one solemn strain!

With pomp of Roman form,
With the grave ritual brought from England's shore,
And with the simple faith which asks no more
Than that the heart be warm!

He, who, till time shall cease,
Will watch that earth, where once, not all in vain,
He died to give us peace, may not disdain
A prayer whose theme is — peace.

Perhaps ere yet the Spring
Hath died into the Summer, over all
The land, the peace of His vast love shall fall,
Like some protecting wing.

Oh, ponder what it means!
Oh, turn the rapturous thought in every way!
Oh, give the vision and the fancy play,
And shape the coming scenes!

Peace in the quiet dales,
Made rankly fertile by the blood of men,
Peace in the woodland, and the lonely glen,
Peace in the peopled vales!

Peace in the crowded town,
Peace in a thousand fields of waving grain,
Peace in the highway and the flowery lane,
Peace on the wind—swept down!

Peace on the farthest seas,
Peace in our sheltered bays and ample streams,
Peace wheresoe'er our starry garland gleams,
And peace in every breeze!

Peace on the whirring marts,
Peace where the scholar thinks, the hunter roams,
Peace, God of Peace! peace, peace, in all our homes,
And peace in all our hearts!

♦

Charleston

Calm as that second summer which precedes
    The first fall of the snow,
In the broad sunlight of heroic deeds,
    The City bides the foe.

As yet, behind their ramparts stern and proud,
    Her bolted thunders sleep—
Dark Sumter, like a battlemented cloud,
    Looms o'er the solemn deep.

No Calpe frowns from lofty cliff or scar
    To guard the holy strand;
But Moultrie holds in leash her dogs of war
    Above the level sand.

And down the dunes a thousand guns lie couched,
    Unseen, beside the flood—
Like tigers in some Orient jungle crouched
    That wait and watch for blood.

Meanwhile, through streets still echoing with trade,
    Walk grave and thoughtful men,
Whose hands may one day wield the patriot's blade
    As lightly as the pen.

And maidens, with such eyes as would grow dim
    Over a bleeding hound,

Seem each one to have caught the strength of him
    Whose sword she sadly bound.

Thus girt without and garrisoned at home,
    Day patient following day,
Old Charleston looks from roof, and spire, and dome,
    Across her tranquil bay.

Ships, through a hundred foes, from Saxon lands
    And spicy Indian ports,
Bring Saxon steel and iron to her hands,
    And Summer to her courts.

But still, along you dim Atlantic Iine,
    The only hostile smoke
Creeps like a harmless mist above the brine,
    From some frail, floating oak.

Shall the Spring dawn, and she still clad in smiles,
    And with an unscathed brow,
Rest in the strong arms of her palm-crowned isles,
    As fair and free as now?

We know not; in the temple of the Fates
    God has inscribed her doom;
And, all untroubled in her faith, she waits
    The triumph or the tomb.

♦

Address Delivered at the Opening
of the New Theatre at Richmond

A fairy ring
Drawn in the crimson of a battle-plain —
From whose weird circle every loathsome thing
And sight and sound of pain
Are banished, while about it in the air,
And from the ground, and from the low-hung skies,
Throng, in a vision fair
As ever lit a prophet's dying eyes,
Gleams of that unseen world
That lies about us, rainbow-tinted shapes
With starry wings unfurled,
Poised for a moment on such airy capes
As pierce the golden foam
Of sunset's silent main —
Would image what in this enchanted dome,
Amid the night of war and death
In which the armed city draws its breath,
We have built up!
For though no wizard wand or magic cup
The spell hath wrought,
Within this charmed fane, we ope the gates
Of that divinest Fairy-land,
Where under loftier fates
Than rule the vulgar earth on which we stand,
Move the bright creatures of the realm of thought.

Shut for one happy evening from the flood
That roars around us, here you may behold —
    As if a desert way
    Could blossom and unfold
    A garden fresh with May —
Substantialised in breathing flesh and blood,
    Souls that upon the poet's page
    Have lived from age to age,
And yet have never donned this mortal clay.
    A golden strand
Shall sometimes spread before you like the isle
    Where fair Miranda's smile
Met the sweet stranger whom the father's art
    Had led unto her heart,
Which, like a bud that waited for the light,
    Burst into bloom at sight!
Love shall grow softer in each maiden's eyes
As Juliet leans her cheek upon her hand,
    And prattles to the night.
    Anon, a reverend form,
    With tattered robe and forehead bare,
That challenge all the torments of the air,
        Goes by!
And the pent feelings choke in one long sigh,
While, as the mimic thunder rolls, you hear
    The noble wreck of Lear
Reproach like things of life the ancient skies,
    And commune with the storm!

Lo! next a dim and silent chamber where,
Wrapt in glad dreams in which, perchance, the Moor
    Tells his strange story o'er,
The gentle Desdemona chastely lies,
Unconscious of the loving murderer nigh.
    Then through a hush like death
    Stalks Denmark's mailed ghost!
And Hamlet enters with that thoughtful breath
Which is the trumpet to a countless host
Of reasons, but which wakes no deed from sleep;
    For while it calls to strife,
He pauses on the very brink of fact
To toy as with the shadow of an act,
And utter those wise saws that cut so deep
    Into the core of life!

    Nor shall be wanting many a scene
    Where forms of more familiar mien,
Moving through lowlier pathways, shall present
    The world of every day,
Such as it whirls along the busy quay,
Or sits beneath a rustic orchard wall,
Or floats about a fashion-freighted hall,
Or toils in attics dark the night away.
Love, hate, grief, joy, gain, glory, shame, shall meet,
As in the round wherein our lives are pent;
    Chance for a while shall seem to reign,
While Goodness roves like Guilt about the street,

And Guilt looks innocent.
But all at last shall vindicate the right,
Crime shall be meted with its proper pain,
Motes shall be taken from the doubter's sight,
And Fortune's general justice rendered plain.
Of honest laughter there shall be no dearth,
Wit shall shake hands with humor grave and sweet,
Our wisdom shall not be too wise for mirth,
Nor kindred follies want a fool to greet.
As sometimes from the meanest spot of earth
A sudden beauty unexpected starts,
So you shall find some germs of hidden worth
    Within the vilest hearts;
And now and then, when in those moods that turn
To the cold Muse that whips a fault with sneers,
You shall, perchance, be strangely touched to learn
    You've struck a spring of tears!

But while we lead you thus from change to change,
Shall we not find within our ample range
Some type to elevate a people's heart —
Some hero who shall teach a hero's part
    In this distracted time?
Rise from thy sleep of ages, noble Tell!
And, with the Alpine thunders of thy voice,
As if across the billows unenthralled
Thy Alps unto the Alleghanies called,
    Bid Liberty rejoice!

Proclaim upon this trans-Atlantic strand
The deeds which, more than their own awful mien,
Make every crag of Switzerland sublime!
And say to those whose feeble souls would lean,
Not on themselves, but on some outstretched hand,
That once a single mind sufficed to quell
The malice of a tyrant; let them know
That each may crowd in every well-aimed blow,
Not the poor strength alone of arm and brand,
But the whole spirit of a mighty land!

Bid Liberty rejoice! Aye, though its day
Be far or near, these clouds shall yet be red
With the large promise of the coming ray.
Meanwhile, with that calm courage which can smile
Amid the terrors of the wildest fray,
Let us among the charms of Art awhile
    Fleet the deep gloom away;
Nor yet forget that on each hand and head
Rest the dear rights for which we fight and pray.

◆

Hymn

(Sung at a sacred concert at Columbia, SC)

FAINT falls the gentle voice of prayer
In the wild sounds that fill the air,
Yet, Lord, we know that voice is heard,
Not less than if Thy throne it stirred.

Thine ear, thou tender One, is caught,
If we but bend the knee in thought;
No choral song that shakes the sky
Floats farther than the Christian's sigh.

Not all the darkness of the land
Can hide the lifted eye and hand;
Nor need the clanging conflict cease,
To make Thee hear our cries for peace.

♦

Carmen Triumphale

Go forth and bid the land rejoice,
Yet not too gladly, 0 my song!
Breathe softly, as if mirth would wrong
The solemn rapture of thy voice.

Be nothing lightly done or said
This happy day! Our joy should flow
Accordant with the lofty woe
That wails above the noble dead.

Let him whose brow and breast were calm
While yet the battle lay with God,
Look down upon the crimson sod
And gravely wear his mournful palm;

And him, whose heart still weak from fear
Beats all too gayly for the time,
Know that intemperate glee is crime
While one dead hero claims a tear.

Yet go thou forth, my song! and thrill,
With sober joy, the troubled days;
A nation's hymn of grateful praise
May not be hushed for private ill.

Our foes are fallen! Flash, ye wires!
The mighty tidings far and nigh!
Ye cities! write them on the sky
In purple and in emerald fires!

They came with many a haughty boast;
Their threats were heard on every breeze;
They darkened half the neighboring seas;
And swooped like vultures on the coast.

False recreants in all knightly strife,
Their way was wet with woman's tears;
Behind them flamed the toil of years,
And bloodshed stained the sheaves of life.

They fought as tyrants fight, or slaves;
God gave the dastards to our hands;
Their bones are bleaching on the sands,
Or mouldering slow in shallow graves.

What though we hear about our path
The heavens with howls of vengeance rent?
The venom of their hate is spent;
We need not heed their fangless wrath.

Meantime the stream they strove to chain
Now drinks a thousand springs, and sweeps
With broadening breast, and mightier deeps,
And rushes onward to the main;

While down the swelling current glides
Our Ship of State before the blast,
With streamers poured from every mast,
Her thunders roaring from her sides.

Lord! bid the frenzied tempest cease,
Hang out thy rainbow on the sea!
Laugh round her, waves! in silver glee,
And speed her to the port of peace!

◆ ◆ ◆

III. English Friends

WILLIAM ERNEST HENLEY (1849–1903) was one of the most prominent English poets of the 19th century, particularly noted for his "*Invictus*." In this poem he speaks in the voice of a British sailor who has run the blockade into Charleston.

Romance

'Talk of pluck!' pursued the Sailor,
Set at euchre on his elbow,
'I was on the wharf at Charleston,
Just ashore from off the runner.

'It was grey and dirty weather,
And I heard a drum go rolling,
Rub—a—dubbing in the distance,
Awful dour—like and defiant.

'In and out among the cotton,
Mud, and chains, and stores, and anchors,
Tramped a squad of battered scarecrows—
Poor old Dixie's bottom dollar!

'Some had shoes, but all had rifles,
Them that wasn't bald was beardless,
And the drum was rolling Dixie,
And they stepped to it like men, sir!

'Rags and tatters, belts and bayonets,
On they swung, the drum a—rolling,
Mum and sour. It looked like fighting,
And they meant it too, by thunder!'

♦ ♦ ♦

PHILIP STANHOPE WORSLEY (1835—1866). Worsley, an English scholar who had translated Homer's *Iliad*, sent General Lee a complimentary copy. On the flyleaf, he inscribed a poem of admiration to the great general:

To GENERAL R. E. LEE, the most stainless of living

commanders, and, except in fortune, the greatest, this

volume is presented with the writer's earnest sympathy

and respectful admiration.

Thy Troy Has Fallen

The grand old bard that never dies,
Receive him in our English tongue!
I send thee, but with weeping eyes,
The story that he sung.

Thy Troy is fallen, thy dear land
Is marred beneath the spoiler's heel.
I cannot trust my trembling hand
To write the things I feel.

Ah, realm of tombs! But let her bear
This blazon to the last of times: —
No nation rose so white and fair,
Or fell so pure of crimes.

The widow's moan, the orphan's wail,
Come round thee; yet in truth be strong!
Eternal right though all else fail,
Can never be made wrong.

An angel's heart, an angel's mouth,
Not Homer's, could alone for me
Hymn well the great Confederate South,
Virginia first, and LEE.

♦ ♦ ♦

SIR HENRY HOUGHTON

A Reply to "The Conquered Banner"

GALLANT nation, foiled by numbers!

Say not that your hopes are fled;

Keep that glorious flag which slumbers,

One day to avenge your dead.

Keep it, widowed, sonless mothers!

Keep it, sisters, mourning brothers!

Furl it with an iron will;

Furl it now but keep it still—

Think not that its work is done.

Keep it till your children take it,

Once again to wail and make it,

All their sires have bled and fought for;

All their noble hearts have sought for—

Bled and fought for all alone.

All alone! ay, shame the story!

Millions here deplore the stain;

Shame, alas! for England's glory,

Freedom called, and called in vain!

Furl that banner sadly, slowly,

Treat it gently, for 'tis holy;

Till that day—yes, furl it sadly;

Then once more unfurl it gladly—

Conquered banner! keep it still!

♦ ♦ ♦

ABOUT THE EDITOR

DR. CLYDE WILSON is Emeritus Distinguished Professor of History of the University of South Carolina, where he served from 1971 to 2006. He holds a Ph.D. from the University of North Carolina at Chapel Hill. He recently completed editing of a 28-volume edition of *The Papers of John C. Calhoun* which has received high praise for quality. He is author or editor of more than 20 other books and over 700 articles, essays, and reviews in a variety of books and journals, and has lectured all over the U.S. and in Europe, many of his lectures having been recorded online and on CDs and DVDs. Dr. Wilson directed 17 doctoral dissertations, a number of which have been published. Books written or edited include *Why the South Will Survive, Carolina Cavalier: The Life and Mind of James Johnston Pettigrew, The Essential Calhoun,* three volumes of *The Dictionary of Literary Biography on* American Historians, *From Union to Empire: Essays in the Jeffersonian Tradition, Defending Dixie: Essays in Southern History and Culture, Chronicles of the South, Calhoun: A Statesman for the 21st Century, The Yankee Problem,* and *Looking For Mr. Jefferson.* Dr. Wilson is founding director of the Society of Independent Southern Historians; former president of the St. George Tucker Society for Southern Studies; recipient of the Bostick Prize for Contributions to South Carolina Letters, the first annual John Randolph Society Lifetime Achievement Award, and of the Robert E. Lee Medal of the Sons of Confederate Veterans. He is M.E. Bradford Distinguished Professor of the Abbeville Institute; Contributing Editor of *Chronicles: A Magazine of American Culture;* founding dean of the Stephen D. Lee Institute, educational arm of the Sons of Confederate Veterans; and co-founder of Shotwell Publishing.

Dr. Wilson has two grown daughters, an excellent son-in-law, and two outstanding grandsons. He lives in the Dutch Fork of South Carolina, not far from the Santee Swamp where Francis Marion and his men rested between raids on the first invader.

JEFFERY ADDICOTT

*Union Terror: Debunking the
False Justifications for Union Terror*

*Trampling Union Terror:
Riders of the Second Alabama Cavalry*

MARK ATKINS

Women in Combat: Feminism Goes to War

JOYCE BENNETT

*Maryland, My Maryland:
The Cultural Cleansing of a Small Southern State*

GARRY BOWERS

*Slavery and The Civil War:
What Your History Teacher Didn't Tell You*

Dixie Days: Reminiscences Of a Southern Boyhood

JERRY BREWER

Dismantling the Republic

ANDREW P. CALHOUN

*My Own Darling Wife: Letters From A
Confederate Volunteer*

JOHN CHODES

Segregation: Federal Policy or Racism?

*Washington's KKK: The Union League During
Southern Reconstruction*

WALTER BRIAN CISCO

War Crimes Against Southern Civilians

DAVID T. CRUM

Stonewall Jackson: Saved by Providence

JOHN DEVANNY

Continuities: The South in a Time of Revolution

*Lincoln's Continuing Revolution: Essays of M.E.
Bradford and Thomas H. Landess*

JOSHUA DOGGRELL

Doxed: The Political Lynching of a Southern Cop

JAMES C. EDWARDS

*What Really Happened?:
Quantrill's Raid On Lawrence, Kansas*

TED EHMANN

*Boom & Bust In Bone Valley: Florida's
Phosphate Mining History 1886-2021*

JOHN AVERY EMISON

*The Deep State Assassination
of Martin Luther King Jr.*

DON GORDON

*Snowball's Chance: My Kidneys Failed,
My Wife Left Me & My Dog Died...*

JOHN R. GRAHAM

Constitutional History of Secession

PAUL C. GRAHAM

Confederaphobia

*When The Yankees Come: Former Carolina
Slaves Remember*

*Nonsense on Stilts: The Gettysburg Address
& Lincoln's Imaginary Nation*

JOE D. HAINES

*The Diary of Col. John Henry Stover Funk
of the Stonewall Brigade, 1861-1862*

CHARLES HAYES

The REAL First Thanksgiving

V.P. HUGHES

Col. John Singleton Mosby: In the News 1862-1916

TERRY HULSEY

25 Texas Heroes

*The Constitution of Non-State Government:
Field Guide to Texas Secession*

JOSEPH JAY

*Sacred Conviction:
The South's Stand for Biblical Authority*

JAMES R. KENNEDY

Dixie Rising: Rules For Rebels

*Nullifying Federal and State Gun Control:
A How-To Guide For Gun Owners*

*When Rebel Was Cool:
Growing Up In Dixie, 1950-1965*

*Reconstruction: Destroying the Republic
and Creating an Empire*

WALTER D. KENNEDY

The South's Struggle: America's Hope

*Lincoln, The Non-Christian President:
Exposing The Myth*

Lincoln, Marx, and the GOP

J.R. & W.D. KENNEDY

*Jefferson Davis: High Road to Emancipation
and Constitutional Government*

*Yankee Empire:
Aggressive Abroad and Despotic at Home*

Punished With Poverty: The Suffering South

The South Was Right! 3rd Edition

LEWIS LIBERMAN

Snowflake Buddies; ABC Leftism For Kids!

PHILIP LEIGH

*The Devil's Town: Hot Springs During
The Gangster Era*

U.S. Grant's Failed Presidency

The Causes of the Civil War

*The Dreadful Frauds: Critical Race Theory
And Identity Politics*

JACK MARQUARDT

*Around The World In 80 Years: Confessions
of a Connecticut Confederate*

MICHAEL MARTIN

Southern Grit: Sensing The Siege at Petersburg

SAMUEL MITCHAM

*The Greatest Lynching In American History:
New York, 1863*

*Confederate Patton: Richard Taylor and
The Red River Campaign*

CHARLES T. PACE

Lincoln As He Really Was

*Southern Independence. Why War? The War
To Prevent Southern Independence*

JAMES R. ROESCH

From Founding Fathers To Fire Eaters

KIRKPATRICK SALE

*Emancipation Hell: The Tragedy Wrought
By Lincoln's Emancipation Proclamation*

JOSEPH SCOTCHIE

*The Asheville Connection:
The Making of a Conservative*

ANNE W. SMITH

Charlottesville Untold: Inside Unite The Right

Robert E. Lee: A History for Kids

KAREN STOKES

A Legion Of Devils: Sherman In South Carolina

*The Burning of Columbia, S.C.: A Review
of Northern Assertions and Southern Facts*

Carolina Love Letters

*Fortunes of War:
The Adventures of a German Confederate*

*A Confederate in Paris:
Letters of A. Dudley Mann 1867-1879*

JOSEPH R. STROMBERG

*Southern Story and Song:
Country Music in the 20th Century*

JACK TROTTER

Last Train to Dixie

JOHN THEURSAM

Key West's Civil War

H.V. TRAYWICK, JR.

*Along The Shadow Line:
A Road Trip through History and Memory
on the Old Confederate Border*

LESLIE TUCKER

*Old Times There Should Not Be Forgotten:
Cultural Genocide In Dixie*

JOHN VINSON

Southerner Take Your Stand!

MARK R. WINCHELL

*Confessions of a Copperhead:
Culture and Politics in the Modern South*

CLYDE N. WILSON

Calhoun: A Statesman for the 21st Century

*Lies My Teacher Told Me: The True History
of the War For Southern Independence*

The Yankee Problem: An American Dilemma

*Annals Of The Stupid Party:
Republicans Before Trump*

*Nullification:
Reclaiming The Consent of the Governed*

The Old South: 50 Essential Books

The War Between The States: 60 Essential Books

*Reconstruction and the New South, 1865-1913:
50 Essential Books*

*The South 20th Century And Beyond:
50 Essential Books*

*Southern Poets and Poems, 1606-1860:
The Land They Loved, Volume 1*

Looking For Mr. Jefferson

African American Slavery in Historical Perspective

JOE WOLVERTON

*What Degree Of Madness?: Madison's Method
To Make American States Again*

WALTER KIRK WOOD

*Beyond Slavery: The Northern Romantic
Nationalist Origins of America's Civil War*

Green Altar (Literary Imprint)

CATHARINE BROSMAN

*An Aesthetic Education
and Other Stories (2nd Ed)*

Chained Tree, Chained Owls: Poems

Aerosols and Other Poems

RANDALL IVEY

*A New England Romance:
And Other Southern Stories*

SUZANNE JOHNSON

Maxcy Gregg's Sporting Journals 1842-1858

JAMES E. KIBBLER, JR.

Tiller : Clayback County Series, Vol. 4

The Gentler Gamester

*In the Deep Heart's Core: Poems of Tribute and
Remembrance (forthcoming)*

THOMAS MOORE

*A Fatal Mercy:
The Man Who Lost The Civil War*

PERRIN LOVETT

The Substitute, Tom Ironsides 1

KAREN STOKES

Belles

Carolina Twilight

Honor in the Dust

The Immortals

The Soldier's Ghost: A Tale of Charleston

WILLIAM THOMAS

*Runaway Haley:
An Imagined Family Saga*

*The Field of Justice: Moonshine
and Murder in North Georgia*

Gold-Bug
(Mystery & Suspense Imprint)

BRANDI PERRY

Splintered: A New Orleans Tale

MARTIN WILSON

To Jekyll and Hide

www.ingramcontent.com/pod-product-compliance
Lightning Source LLC
Chambersburg PA
CBHW052354060726

47592CB00020B/2220